Turning
the
Diamond

After some years with the Overseas Missionary Fellowship
in Thailand, the Revd Dennis Lennon was ordained into the
Church of England. He served at the Round Church, and
then at St Barnabas, both in Cambridge. From St Thomas
Episcopal Church in Edinburgh, notable for its church
planting experiments, he moved to Sheffield to become
Diocesan Adviser in Evangelism. Dennis is married and
has two children.

D1388075

Turning
the
Diamond

Exploring George Herbert's
Images of Prayer

Dennis Lennon

For Ruth y Patrick

Published in Great Britain in 2002
Society for Promoting Christian Knowledge
Holy Trinity Church
Marylebone Road
London NW1 4DU

British Library Cataloguing-in-Publication Data

A catalogue record for this book is available from the British Library

ISBN 0-281-05470-3

Typeset by Pioneer Associates, Perthshire
Printed in Great Britain by
Antony Rowe Ltd, Chippenham, Wiltshire

Contents

Prayer

Prayer the Church's banquet, Angels' age,
   God's breath in man returning to his birth,
   The soul in paraphrase, heart in pilgrimage,
The Christian plummet sounding heaven and earth;

Engine against the Almighty, sinner's tower,
   Reversed thunder, Christ-side-piercing spear,
   The six-days world transposing in an hour,
A kind of tune, which all things hear and fear;

Softness, and peace, and joy, and love, and bliss,
   Exalted Manna, gladness of the best,
   Heaven in ordinary, man well dressed,
The Milky Way, the bird of Paradise,

Church-bells beyond the stars heard, the soul's blood,
The land of spices; something understood.

CHAPTER 1

On finding a diamond

When the supervisor of a household rubbish-tip exercises her inalienable right to trawl through the day's deposits for any items of worth, delicious surprises lurk. She appeared last evening on television with a few of her recent finds for an expert to examine. Pieces of jewellery, they were, lifted out from among heaps of old newspapers, stale bread and broken crockery. Our expert was taken with one necklace in particular, which he judged to be 'Unusual . . . very beautiful. This would fetch around six thousand pounds.' There is something satisfying in the idea of diamonds born-again from a rubbish-dump.

I found, buried under a pile of junk on a market stall in Fulham, a copy of George Herbert's poems, beautifully signed inside, 'Lilian M. Lamb. July 1888.' I still have her book and wish she could know how much it means to me. Perhaps she does. It appeared in the nick of time because my attempts to make a go of the Christian life were floundering and I was struggling to stay connected. I recall the moment like this: standing at that stall looking for nothing in particular, when the Holy Spirit nudged my attention in the right direction and whispered, 'Try George Herbert.' I did. I still do.

'If I read a book and I feel physically as if the top of my head were taken off, I know that is poetry . . . is there any other way?' So Emily Dickinson described her own intuitive test of poetry. George Herbert can have a similar effect on people. For myself, I had not realized before that biblical orthodoxy was allowed to be so beautiful, luminous with love and delight in God. Or that serious things could be expressed with such charm, and high doctrine considered with meditative playfulness. Neither had I been aware that a person's relationship with the Lord Jesus Christ could be this robust, sincere and transparent, as between two dear friends.

1

Perhaps now is the moment to turn to the subject of this small book. Please read, a couple of times, and slowly if you will, Herbert's extraordinary sonnet 'Prayer'. Doesn't it leave you feeling just slightly scalped? After years of pondering it, I still come away thinking, 'If this is prayer, then I know nothing about prayer.' Its strange, exuberant, shimmering joy and the haunting imagery – isn't it quite unlike anything else you have read on prayer? I promise you, it will refresh anyone's jaded prayer-life.

'The poem is an inspired litany... this zodiac of marvels'[1] is spell-binding as it leads from the condoned spiritual violence of prayer (in lines five and six) directed at heaven and against the cosmic principalities and powers, through to those magical final three lines whose 'near-hallucinogenic intensity'[2] takes the reader out of all thought.

The sonnet is made up of some 27 metaphors and images (a single word may be emblematic), each one a symbol of a point in our experience of prayer. It is like a diamond with 27 facets; 27 doors left on the latch for the seeker to enter and, following with a meditative imagination, to explore the prayer-country beyond; which is to say, to enter prayer from fresh directions.

It amounts to a jewel-like vision of prayer as not simply one aspect of a larger Christian experience (which is how it is commonly regarded) but as a synonym for living in God – as all-inclusive of our total existence as that. It is a vision, which exposes our own prayerlessness for what it is, a bizarre disorder, a self-inflicted starvation – a jewel thrown on to a rubbish-tip.

George Herbert (1593–1633) was a mystic with both feet on the ground, full of 'daylight sanity and vigour'.[3] Within the ferocious religious turmoil of his day he stood about halfway between Puritan and Catholic. In 'his via media between preciousness and vulgarity... George Herbert exemplified the body heat of healthy Anglican life'.[4] A brilliantly gifted high-flyer and an aristocratic academic, Herbert was an excellent Latin and Greek scholar and spoke Italian, French and Spanish. He was Public Orator at Cambridge University, a Member of Parliament, and an accomplished musician. But the key to Herbert lies in the fact that he was, first and last, Christ's man ('my doctrine tuned by Christ').

On finding a diamond

In 1626 the course of his life dramatically altered when he turned from pursuing a glittering career, resigned his seat in Parliament and was ordained in the Church of England, becoming Rector of Bemerton, a small rural parish on the edge of Salisbury, in 1630. Three years later, at the age of 40, George Herbert was dead.

Some may have a problem with a creation such as 'Prayer', or rather, with its creator. They wonder, is this *real*, or was Herbert just a spiritual romantic who happened to have a bewitching way with beautiful words – is he just saying things?

Two aspects of Herbert's short but remarkable ministry at Bemerton speak in answer to those misgivings: his approach to preaching, and his pastoral wisdom. Herbert quickly realized that a preaching style and method appropriate for Cambridge were useless at Bemerton. Long sermons peppered with classical references were worse than irrelevant for people struggling daily to keep body and soul together. Anyway, for Herbert, the whole point of preaching and teaching was not interest or even edification, but growth in prayer. Does the sermon or Bible study leave people more motivated and equipped to pray? He advises:

> Resort to sermons, but to prayer most:
> Praying's the end of preaching.

Something of a spiritual revival occurred in the Bemerton district under Herbert's teaching. His biographer Izaak Walton records that farm workers 'did so love and respect Mr. Herbert that they would let their plough rest when Mr. Herbert's Saints Bell rang to prayers, that they might also offer their devotions to God with him; and would then return back to their plough'.

George Herbert found his 'Bemerton' model for communication in that great medieval teaching visual aid, the stained glass church window with its faith-stories 'annealed in glass'. He prayed to become 'a window, through thy grace', a living, breathing, walking embodiment of the gospel irradiated by the light of the Holy Spirit for all to see and learn.

Lord, how can man preach thy eternal word?
 He is a brittle crazy glass:
Yet in thy temple thou dost him afford
  This glorious and transcendent place,
  To be a window, through thy grace.

But when thou dost anneal in glass thy story,
  Making thy life to shine within
The holy Preacher's; then the light and glory
  More rev'rend grows, and more doth win:
  Which else shows wat'rish, bleak, and thin.

Doctrine and life, colours and light, in one
  When they combine and mingle, bring
A strong regard and awe: but speech alone
  Doth vanish like a flaring thing,
  And in the ear, not conscience ring.

('The Windows')

By the time of his death, Herbert's consideration for people, and in particular his practical care for the poor, were proverbial. You can still see his parting message, addressed 'to my successor', an inscription above the porch at the front of Bemerton Rectory, which he rebuilt largely at his own expense:

If thou chance for to find
A new house to thy mind,
And built without thy cost:
Be good to the poor,
As God gives thee store,
And then, my labour's not lost.

Herbert's writings are permeated with rich pastoral wisdom, mostly hard-won from his struggle with being the person he was. Aldous Huxley called him our poet of 'inner weather', meaning not the lovely reliable Californian variety, but our changeable, unpredictable, drizzle–sun–fog British weather. It seems he was troubled all his life with the effects of dramatic swings in his psychological and spiritual ups-and-downs; from ecstasy to despair and all the way back up again, he tells us, within the space of an hour. He sought God, and was found by him, within the inner roller coaster of light and dark, warmth and cold, joy and misery.

> Ah my dear angry Lord,
> Since thou dost love, yet strike;
> Cast down, yet help afford;
> Sure I will do the like.
>
> I will complain, yet praise;
> I will bewail, approve:
> And all my sour-sweet days
> I will lament, and love.
> ('Bitter-Sweet')

Out of it came a saving insight, namely, that although we can no more escape our temperament than we can jump out of our skin, it is also true that our temperament cannot escape the grasp of the God of love. It is love, God's love for us and our answering love for him (see how they touch in the third line of the verse quoted below, from the poem 'The Temper') which masters and redeems the present moment, in whatever form or mood it may come upon us, making always 'one place ev'ry where'.

> Whether I fly with angels, fall with dust,
> Thy hands made both, and I am there:
> Thy power and love, my love and trust
> Make one place ev'ry where.

Perhaps these brief references to George Herbert's ministry are sufficient to suggest the reality of a man whose spirituality bears the tool-marks of costly devotion to Christ and his people. The writings are the fruit of the man he was. His deeply experiencing mind and experimental faith pushed at the boundaries of the believer's life in Christ.

He was like that man in Jesus' metaphor of the treasure-room (Matthew 13.52): 'Therefore every teacher of the law who has been instructed about the kingdom of heaven is like the owner of a house who brings out of his storeroom new treasures as well as old.' Notice, not 'up-to-date' and 'old-fashioned' treasures, but *new* expressions and applications of what is an *eternal* wisdom. Can 'Prayer', written in the 1600s, have serious relevance for us today? What a typically modern sort of question that is! Rather we should ask if 'Prayer' holds eternal things, for 'to be always relevant you must say things that are eternal' (Simone Weil). Only by penetrating 'Prayer' and practising its wisdom will we see if it deals in eternal things.

If we were to approach Herbert's house (thinking now of Jesus' metaphor) in search of spiritual resources for a Christian life under today's spiritually stressful conditions, my guess is that he would have us weighed and measured with a glance. He would notice the tell-tale signs of our spiritual exhaustion and quiet despair, which derive from our terminal self-reliance; our unbridled restlessness; and the worldliness, which leaves the super-structure of our faith intact while eating out its heart and lungs. I believe George Herbert, wise pastor, would disappear into that storeroom of his at the back of the house and emerge with 'Prayer' for our renewal.

As we explore his images it matters with what slant of mind we come to the task. Not with a problem-solving attitude as if we were attempting to demystify some of the exhibits at the Tate Modern gallery, or to solve tricky mental arithmetic. We will simply stand before each symbol and invite it to lead us. Therefore, no haste. Be ready for an image to reach out to you with particular urgency because it coincides with your situation at that moment. Then drop all else and go with it.

By saying 'go with it' we mean allow one insight to connect with the next and so lead your meditation out on to fresh ground. The secret lies in turning the insights and disclosures over and over in your meditative thinking. The particular line of thought given in each chapter is no more than that, one line of thought to get meditation and prayer under way; a kick-start, nothing more. The real pleasure will lie in your own grasping of the symbol, when you find yourself saying, for example, 'Well, yes, fair enough, but it seems to me that to say prayer is "the land of spices" is also suggesting this . . . and this.' Always our purpose in each chapter is the enlargement and the empowering of our practice of prayer.

We have spoken as though getting into Herbert's ideas will be wholly of our doing, as if by our powers of close attention we will be able to squeeze until they yield up their essence. But C. S. Lewis points out that the necessary condition of all good reading is 'to get ourselves out of the way', and that the first step towards a work of art is *surrender*.[5] The questions to ask are not, 'What am I looking for in these words? What can I get from them to help me better understand prayer?' but, 'What are these words looking for in me? How do they read me? What is revealed as I surrender my prayer-life to their scrutiny?' Which, of course, is how we were taught to read scripture.

Finally, and before we turn to exploring what 'Prayer the Church's banquet, Angels' age' might mean for us, two suggestions: first, that you keep a note-book record of how your thought and prayer develop, and, second, that you memorize the sonnet. Its unusual and vivid character makes it surprisingly memory-friendly; you will then 'have it by heart' for life, which is even better than having it on the page. As your inward possession, written upon the walls of your mind and available to your imagination, 'Prayer' will work for you as a spring of meditation and prayer.

We will discover our brother George Herbert to be a master at prayer. We have his diamond. Turn it in the light.

CHAPTER 2

Prayer the Church's banquet, Angels' age

'Prayer the Church's banquet,' says George Herbert, at which a few us will mutter, 'Not in my experience, it isn't.' A sense of duty, rather than a sense of feasting, is what drives our prayer. Sure, we have our champagne moments when heaven and earth touch, but for the most part we pray because Jesus says we should. Our Lord prayed as if his life depended upon it, how much more should we. He commands, 'Pray continually' (1 Thessalonians 5.17), which should be enough for any Christian. In church on a Sunday we expect prayers for the world (it is our duty) regardless of the feelings of those leading the intercessions, or the mood of the congregation. Duty out-ranks whim every time. What more is there to say? Only this: experience reveals the downward spiral of duty. Duty can become *mere* duty, then *grim* duty, and even *empty* duty, as we routinely crank the prayer-mill over and over again.

Mention banqueting and Herbert's imagination leaps to the angels. Far older than human experience of it, prayer is as old as 'Angels' age'. Our banqueting takes place among glorious beings who have been at the business of prayer since their creation and long before ours. When God 'laid the earth's cornerstone – the morning stars sang together and all the angels shouted for joy' (Job 38.6, 7). We pray, and our words enter a cosmos already pulsating with angelic adoration. The sound of their voices rocked the great temple to its foundations and frightened the prophet out of his wits (Isaiah 6.1–4), a symbol of a universe set shuddering on its axis by their worship. With angels Herbert is sketching in the context, the environment within which we pray. 'You have come to Mount Zion (*now, already*), to the heavenly Jerusalem, the city of the living God.

You have come (*now, already*) to thousands upon thousands of angels in joyful assembly' (Hebrews 12.22). Another translation has 'we have come before countless angels making festival'. Not only after we die and move over into eternity but now, already, 'you have come' into the angelic festival. Among such an irresistible company of friends prayer can only be a banquet.

But without the assurance of a surrounding company we would be left to ourselves, tinkering about with our moods in an attempt to work up a sense that we are not alone. How do you cope with the 'empty room' test each morning? Perhaps I am alone in this but let me explain how it goes. We wake up in the morning and attempt to greet the Lord in prayer. But at that moment our mood is largely determined by a sense that the room is empty. We feel we are praying into an empty, neutral space with God, if anywhere, on the far side of the space. Set down on paper these 'impressions on waking up' seem childish and banal yet they do express a primitive and stubborn anxiety, which subverts joy in prayer: is the room as empty as it looks? You can extend and apply the 'empty room' metaphor to every sphere of life.

First, the truth about the room is not to be found in how we feel about it, but in God's word on the subject. The room exists within a holy sphere teeming with angelic presence, those 'countless angels making festival'. As for our poor old bemused and fluctuating feelings, they will, eventually, catch up with revelation and be warmed and delighted with the truth. We pray within the innumerable angelic company whose very existence since their creation is for prayer. A magic word for the early Christians was *isangelos* – 'equal to the angels'. They envied the angels their ability to live to God every moment and not let a single drop of grace go to waste.[1]

Yet we remain, for the most part, stubbornly secular and closed-off to the reality of angels. Centuries of their misrepresentation by the devotional kitsch industry have blighted our angel-imagination. We find it difficult to take them seriously. Look in any churchyard: anaemic young people draped in bed-sheets, and equipped with hopelessly inadequate wings, pass for ministering angels on the graves. Sweet, sentimental, inoffensive, and not a bit like that figure of immense weight and dazzling radiance John saw '. . . coming down from heaven. He was robed in a cloud, with a rainbow above his head; his face was like the sun, and his legs were like fiery pillars . . . He planted his right foot on the sea and his left foot on the land, and he gave a loud shout like the roar of a lion. When he shouted, the voices of seven thunders spoke' (Revelation 10.1–3). Difficult to imagine such a being tethered at great-aunt Betty's tombstone.

The spiritual writer Ladislaus Boros comments in similar vein:

> the angels . . . are so far above everything human that when they enter our realm of existence they tend to threaten us by the very majesty of their being. They are the light and ardour of creation, and the essence of all feeling and emotion. They are worshippers of the most profoundly concentrated power. They are searchers of the depths of divinity. They straddle, plumb and span the whole realm of earth. In the area of human existence an angel is universally pervasive and penetrative; we conceive of their power as an angel's ability to fly.[2]

Imagine these for your partners in prayer!

That those spiritual realities may become real to us, in our 'empty rooms', the apostle Paul prayed 'that the eyes of your heart may be enlightened' (Ephesians 1.17–19). We need a Dothan-esque encounter. At Dothan Israel's enemy, the King of Aram, attempted to capture the prophet Elisha:

> When the servant of the man of God got up and went out early the next morning, an army with horses and chariots had surrounded the city. 'Oh, my lord, what shall we do?' the servant asked. 'Don't be afraid,' the prophet answered. 'Those who are with us are more than those who are with them.' And Elisha prayed, 'O LORD, open his eyes so that he may see.' Then the LORD opened the servant's eyes, and he looked and saw the hills full of horses and chariots of fire all round Elisha. (2 Kings 6.15–17)

If we are among such powers when we pray, then clearly the gloomy threat of the empty room vanishes. We now see it for what it is, a lie put about by the dark powers disturbed by the sight of Christians praying effectively. To be on the side of the angels (and what a world of meaning resides in that throw-away cliché) means that the balance of power has shifted decisively and irreversibly our way. We say this regardless of how many, or how few, attended last night's prayer meeting or were in church last Sunday. It must be for this reason we can find in the New Testament no reflection of our own almost neurotic preoccupation with the size of congregations. Because we have the holy 'principalities and powers' with us it's all up with the numbers game. Small, unimportant and often persecuted churches scattered around Asia Minor went cheerfully about their calling to be the light of the world, Imperial Rome's world, in the knowledge that they lived with all heaven about them (Acts 7.55, 56). As we pray in Christ, heaven and this world stand open to each other. Consider this stunning vision of spiritual violence unleashed against evil powers on earth when Christians pray and engage with the great angels at the throne of God:

> When he opened the seventh seal, there was silence in heaven for about half an hour. And I saw the seven angels who stand before God, and to them were given seven trumpets. Another angel, who had a golden censer, came and stood at the altar. He was given much incense to offer, with the prayers of all the saints, on the golden altar before the throne. The smoke of the incense, together with the prayers of the saints, went up before God from the angel's hand. Then the angel took the censer, filled it with fire from the altar, and hurled it on the earth; and there came peals of thunder, rumblings, flashes of lightning and an earthquake. (Revelation 8.1–5)

In the heavenlies of 'the Revelation' the cosmic din is deafening. God turns down the volume, 'silence for about half an hour', so that the prayers of his people may come up to him. The result is awesome. Prayers from those small churches release dangerous and subversive powers back into the world. The great Angel-Priest has scooped into his censer blazing coals from off the altar of incense, he swings it around to fan the fire before hurling the contents

11

back on to the heads of God's enemies; the *size* of the praying congregation is beside the point. They are pictured as protected from the fiery shower by the seal of God's name on their foreheads (Revelation 7.3). The resulting conflagration and panic are described in classic terms of apocalyptic pyrotechnics.

Who are these potent Christians whose prayers can engage the powers of God's great angels? Small, anonymous groups, by no means perfect, living under the hostile gaze of the most powerful pagan regime the world had known. A simple action like a pinch of incense in the flame at the public shrine to Caesar would be enough to keep a Christian on the safe side of the Imperial authorities. But these people know of another flame at another altar and the incense of prayer in Christ's name.

As the angel of the altar answers their prayers, those congregations are moving from the margins of world affairs into their centre. Prayer ducks under the façade of things to reach to the heart, it puts the believer in touch with the deep mystery of historical processes and events. We tend to regard prayer as an exercise in clearing up trouble and mess in society; like a fire engine, or one of those street-cleaning carts, scurrying about to douse fires and make things better. But the praying churches of 'the Revelation' were the real aggressors: they were the arsonists. Their prayers set the earth ablaze with the dangerous fires of God's purposes.

How can we learn this fire-of-God quality? In terms of that scene around the golden altar, the answer to our question is in the quality of the incense. Christ is himself the incense, 'a fragrant offering' (Ephesians 5.2). The smoke of the incense from the angel's hand went up before God with his people's prayers. The incense cloud opens up to admit the words, enfolds and accompanies the prayed words up to the presence of the Father. Christ is the lovely aroma of incense, which perfumes our words. It is not possible to separate and distinguish the aroma from the words as they ascend as one.

Thus Jesus prays ceaselessly for his people, and not only *for* us: he gathers our prayers into his and offers them, as one, to the Father. He opens up his prayers so that ours can enter his, and participate in his, as his. He takes up our confused mumblings and splutterings ('we do not know what we ought to pray for'

(Romans 8.26), so that our voice mingles with his voice as we 'pray through the mouth of Christ' (Calvin). In him our poor prayers are sorted out, unscrambled, interpreted, cleansed, redeemed and made effective as they are raised on the power of his prayer: irresistible to the Father.

In this symbolism Christ is the Angel-Priest at the altar who both offers the incense of adoration and intercession, *and* brings 'fire on the earth' (Luke 12.49). This mysterious process of boundlessly gracious power and love is indicated by the image of Christ as our great High Priest, and in the familiar conclusion to prayer: 'These things we ask in the name of Jesus. Amen.'

'Angels' age', or Adam's age – we are set the same exhilarating challenge for which both angels and humans were created and which justifies the existence of all things: how to adore God adequately; how to keep up with the runaway beauty and love of God: 'When you praise the Lord, exalt him as much as you can, for he will surpass even that. When you exalt him, put forth all your strength, and do not grow weary, for you cannot praise him enough. Who has seen him and can describe him? Or who can extol him as he is?'[3]

Only love can rise to this challenge; duty will never do it, it hasn't the motivation or the imagination. Duty will cause us to do things well, and to pray conscientiously, but only love will do it beautifully, totally. When love is in the ascendancy, prayer escapes from mere dutifulness, techniques and time-slots, like a bird flying its cage. Love confers on our praying the character of a banquet. Give Love an inch and before you can turn around she is 'weaving plainsong into a garland'. The spiritual writer Urs von Balthasar describes the simplicity at the heart of banquet-prayer: 'God is no trainer of souls bent on attaining extravagant record performances. He is a lover who wants nothing but great love and who accepts with a smile anything such a love invents to offer him.'[4] In those words we see the candlelight, hear the laughter and music, and smell the aromas of superb food: it is a banquet.

Von Balthasar's picture brings to mind the lovely way parents will give pride of place – on kitchen walls, or at the office – to those simple little daubs dashed off with such confidence, and presented with complete assurance for parental praise, by their small children. 'Paintings', which are quite worthless, are mysteriously drawn into the realm of the priceless. Child-love makes and offers; parent-love is delighted to accept and treasure the gift. Within that exchange of love is what George Herbert means by 'Prayer the Church's banquet':

> Wherefore with my utmost art
> I will sing thee,
> And the cream of all my heart
> I will bring thee.
>
> ('Praise' 2)

This simple analogy of giving and receiving, between child and parent, illuminates also the opposite condition of our bland and unconvincing prayer-life. The joy, freedom and exuberance of the banquet (and without them banqueting is not possible, we would be left with a meal no more exciting than the Firm's Annual Dinner) are born out of confidence, security and trust. We are up against our deeply embedded doubts and fears about God. Prayer as banquet, in the full-blooded sense, sounds to our suspicious ears just too good to be true. We feel beggars belong in the street, so even when we hear the Lord's 'Welcome – come in!' we stay outside the banquet looking in through the window. We can hardly bring ourselves to embrace it and act upon it. Our instincts are to stand in the corner, to stay at the level of duty, which comes more naturally to us. George MacDonald said, 'It is the heart that is not yet sure of its God that is afraid to laugh in his presence.'[5] Like the Prodigal Son, 'I am no longer worthy to be called your son; make me like one of your hired men' (Luke 15.19).

It occurred to me only quite recently, in a moment of maudlin reflection, that in my childhood every time my father looked at me he smiled. Even though for some of that time we were dodging bombs in the London Blitz, with half the neighbourhood going up in flames, I recall it in terms of complete security, within my parents' love and commitment. A sense of banquet-in-the-Blitz!

Prayer will come out of the shadows and into the joy of the feast, when our insecurities and suspicions in relation to God are answered and laid to rest. George Herbert is still with us in this for in his own way he passed through the same crisis. His answer is exquisite in its courtesy, and profoundly satisfying to the clamouring conscience. Prayer will become banquet once we allow ourselves to be entertained at *another* feast. Not a feast of our making but one prepared, financed, hosted, and serviced by Christ. First, allow yourself (and this can be so difficult) to be welcomed and seated by him at his table. Again, love is the Master of Ceremonies, and this love will not take our refusal for an answer:

Love 3

Love bade me welcome: yet my soul drew back,
      Guilty of dust and sin.
But quick-eyed Love, observing me grow slack
      From my first entrance in,
Drew nearer to me, sweetly questioning,
      If I lacked anything.

A guest, I answered, worthy to be here:
      Love said, You shall be he.
I the unkind, ungrateful? Ah my dear,
      I cannot look on thee.
Love took my hand, and smiling did reply,
      Who made the eyes but I?

Truth Lord, but I have marred them: let my shame
      Go where it doth deserve.
And know you not, says Love, who bore the blame?
      My dear, then I will serve.
You must sit down, says Love, and taste my meat:
      So I did sit and eat.

At this feast, the causes of our unrest are traced down to their roots: 'guilt – dust – sin – unkindness – ingratitude – marred – shame'. Traced, named, exposed, and then cancelled by Christ who 'bore the blame' in his death on the cross when he gave himself to become the life of the world.

This feast belongs with that series of reconciliation-meals in the Gospels leading to the Passover meal at the Last Supper, and pointing forward to 'the wedding supper of the Lamb' (Revelation 19.9) at the End-Time. In the biblical tradition, the quality of the meal, the exuberant hospitality, the warmth of friendship and compelling courtesy of it all symbolize our Lord's pleasure at our company. You are the apple of his eye (Psalm 17.8): 'Sit and eat.'

Christ hosts the feast, and of course he *is* the feast, he 'bore the blame'. Out of that communion with him there arises a spiritual chemistry, which transforms whatever it touches into gratitude. Without gratitude energizing our prayers they will always be susceptible to distortion by ulterior motives: the sneak glance in the mirror, the self-satisfied smirk that says, 'Look how beautifully I pray! How spiritual I am.' But gratitude looks out to the one who 'bore the blame'; it is self-forgetful in its adoration of the saviour. And gratitude gives the most original parties!

Does this beg the question? If gratitude is the catalyst for that banqueting, which is the Church's prayer, how shall I become a grateful person? I cannot talk or beat myself into it as a state of mind. George Herbert knows that gratitude is in the gift of God. Only he can get under the root of our being by his Holy Spirit and there pour in gratitude. It is a case of, 'Lord, command what you will, and give what you command' (Origen). In his delightful way Herbert corners God with this ultimatum: along with all your other gifts you must give gratitude also or you will lose the lot!

> Thou that hast giv'n so much to me,
> Give one thing more, a grateful heart.
> See how thy beggar works on thee
> By art.

He makes thy gifts occasion more
And says, if he in this be crossed,
All thou hast giv'n him heretofore
    Is lost . . .

Wherefore I cry, and cry again,
And in no quiet canst thou be
Till I a thankful heart obtain
    Of Thee:

Not thankful, when it pleaseth me;
As if thy blessings had spare days:
But such a heart, whose pulse may be
    Thy praise.
                ('Gratefulness')

If prayer is the Church's banquet, then prayer is not so much the self-expression of the Church as its nourishment. The evidence is everywhere, in our congregations, and in our personal lives: without prayer we become spiritually malnourished, frail, anxious about ourselves like sick people. But the promise in this, George Herbert's first image, is of people confident in God, flourishing in banquet-prayer, with 'a heart whose pulse may be thy praise'.

CHAPTER 3

God's breath in man returning to his birth

The first sparkle from George Herbert's diamond gave exotic images of prayer as feasting, and as angelic longevity. The second facet of his stone could not be more different in its plain simplicity: prayer is like breathing. It is 'God's breath in man returning to his birth'. This is prayer as rejuvenation.

Nothing is more elusive than the over-familiar, well-worn thing. 'Breathing' is a humdrum, thirty-thousand-times-a-day activity and thereby virtually impenetrable to the imagination. Like a powerful blowtorch burning off skin upon skin of old paint, scripture comes to our aid with the picture of Adam (ourselves) as a 'living being' because God 'breathed into his nostrils the breath of life' (Genesis 2.7). God inspired his child with his own breath, his divine vital power, when he stooped down to impart the first kiss of life.

The Hebrew scholar Lawrence Kushner makes a fascinating suggestion about our ability to breathe. He invites us to listen to the soft sighing our breathing makes, and he relates the sound to the divine name in the Hebrew text, which cannot be pronounced as written.

> The four letters of the Name of God are yod, hay, vav, and hay. They are frequently mispronounced as Yahveh. But in truth they are unutterable. Not because of the holiness they evoke, but because they are all vowels and you cannot pronounce all the vowels at once without risking respiratory injury. *This word is the sound of breathing.* The holiest Name in the world, the Name of the creator, is the sound of your own breathing.[1]

That sort of semi-mystical interpretation either leaves you cold ('those old Rabbis at it again! Staring too long at the text'), or you may find it suggestive and moving. To think that God placed the sound of his unknowable Name on the breath of every man, woman and child. Quite unconsciously, day and night, we sigh the unutterable name. It is a use of 'God's breath in man' which sends it back to 'his birth' in God: a wonderful sign of the creator's closeness to his children. How near is God to you? Listen for the sound of the breath in your body.

If you are taken with this interpretation of breath as a symbol of the divine presence (and the unutterable Name means something like 'the one who brings into being all that is') you may wish to follow it further in this exercise described by Lawrence Kushner:

> Find a place and a time that are quiet enough to hear the sound of your own breathing. Simply listen to that barely audible noise and intend that with each inhalation and exhalation you sound the Name of Being. It may be no accident that this exercise is universally acknowledged as an easy and effective method for focussing and relaxation.[2]

Our breath comes to us as the Father's gift and returns to him when freighted with our prayer, love and praise. The fact that we live in complete moment-by-moment dependence upon the vital power of 'God's breath in man' means that we will understand our existence when we see it as giftedness. The fact that we are breathing, at this moment, is the ever-present reminder of our utter indebtedness to God. Thanksgiving becomes a driving force within us. We breathe, we lift up our voices in prayer; our breathing follows the great doxological contour: 'For from God and through him and to him are all things. To him be the glory for ever! Amen' (Romans 11.36).

Prayer is thus the most normal and natural use of our breath. The act of prayer throws open the windows of our interior world, ventilating our spirit, allowing our breath to surge through us and out on its short return journey to God. Here is the homing instinct of the prayers we breathe; like a child running to her mother's arms; like a magnetic needle searching about until it settles on north.

Thee, God, I come from, to thee go,
All day long I like fountain flow
From thy hand out, swayed about
Mote-like in thy mighty glow.

(Hopkins)[3]

Conversely, consider the stress placed on our spirits whenever we neglect or suppress prayer. Remarking on the spiritual and psychological harm we may cause ourselves and others if we deny prayer, G. K. Chesterton warns:

Beware the danger of insolence, of being too big for our boots...The gesture of worship is generous and beautiful... henceforth anything that takes away the gesture of worship stunts and even maims us forever. Henceforth being merely secular is servitude and inhibition. If we cannot pray we are gagged; if we cannot kneel we are in irons.[4]

Society would be a happier and healthier place if it accepted prayer as normal, natural, ordinary, as necessary to a person's well being as the rain and sun, and not as a special religious interest. Although some two-thirds of the population in surveys claim to 'pray often', it is accompanied with a confession of a sense of embarrassment in admitting as much to others. There is something about the prevailing secular scepticism which battens down on our urge to pray.

So far, in following Herbert's metaphor, we have thought of breathing as making speech, prayer and praise, possible for us. But of course breath is the vital power of our entire bodily life, and properly understood our entire bodily life comes into play when we pray. Prayer is the total response of the whole person to God within the full range of lived experience. In Abraham Kuyper's words, 'There is not an inch of any sphere of life to which Jesus Christ the Lord does not say "mine!"' Chesterton was looking for something wider than speech in his defence of 'the gesture of worship' which we will want to take in its most comprehensive sense. 'God's breath in man' fulfils its mission when the entire life in the body is offered to God, including speech.

Consider why Jesus the Son of God took a body when he entered the life of the world as its saviour. We can imagine more powerful, less confined and limited forms in which he could have come for his work of salvation. Given the immensity of his task, was it wise to come as a baby? But only that form would do. God looks for the response of love from his human family, and in order to redeem us from the catastrophe of our appalling un-love, the Son must offer perfect love and obedience from within a human body, as one of us. Therefore 'a body you prepared for me . . . I have come to do your will, O God' (Hebrews 10.5, 7). Can God be glorified by a free-choosing human being, offering himself in every aspect of his humanity? That was Jesus' task. He came 'to do your will, O God', for which purpose it was 'a body you prepared for me', as our representative brother.

Think of the will of God for each of us as a piece of music, written personally by a composer who knows each one's distinctive instrument. That instrument is your uniquely designed and gifted body, energized by 'God's breath in man', intended for communion with God in a relationship of love. Nothing else will serve as an instrument on which to interpret and perform the music. 'Sacrifices and offerings you did not desire,' said Jesus, because they are less than the image of God.

From within the gifts and powers of our bodily life we offer prayer and praise to the Father by living our lives in his will; playing the music he has set for us. In the free, glad, full offering of your bodily life you live out your prayer. Music has the mysterious power both to hold the performer under its discipline (or under its spell if you prefer) while at the same time releasing her to interpret and play to the very limits of her skill. God asks no more from us, and in love we cannot offer him less. There is a will of God for every moment. We are never more true to ourselves than when we are living the will of God. It is equally true that we cannot live the will of God unless we are our true selves. Prayer is as wide, as deep, and as totally inclusive of our bodily existence as that. If we can use such a phrase, the most comprehensive level of prayer is 'behaviour-prayer'.

Prayer calls into play all our powers of imagination and invention in the choices it makes. The word of God, by which we learn of the will of God, can only bring us to the starting line and point us in the right direction at the beginning of the race. For example, the will of God is always that we 'love one another as Christ has loved us'. That is the starting line. But from there on into the race it is up to each of us to decide how we interpret and enact the command; how we experiment with it, seeking fresh expressions of that love, the risks, the innovation, the sacrifice, the outlay of our resources – we decide. 'The breath of God in man' is given us for that end, a breath that can 'return to its birth' as our decisions are made in the service of love.

Prayer lived out through the entirety of bodily life transcends those artificial partitions by which we divide up our discipleship (e.g. into Bible reading, church, witness, service, mission, etc.). Behaviour-prayer reintegrates our trivialized and fragmented personal world because now everything connects as a cause for prayer; everything relates around the centre of Christ's love.

But are we still missing something in Herbert's words? By now we know enough of his thoughts to expect rich subtleties and depths within his apparent simplicities. The idea of breath returning to 'his birth' is puzzling. Breath, after we have done with it, is normally exhaled to its 'death' not its birth. When it has fulfilled its mission and spent itself delivering its oxygen to keep us ticking over a little longer, breath is finished. Exhaled, it is absorbed back into the atmosphere.

But prayer, Herbert says, reverses that natural process of deterioration and exhaustion, which leads to the 'death of breath'. Prayer takes it back the other way to 'his birth', the place of regeneration and new beginnings. *Prayer is the agent of rejuvenation because it puts the one who prays into communion with the risen Christ, the Lord of life.* 'He . . . set his seal of ownership on us, and put his Spirit in our hearts as a deposit, guaranteeing what is to come' (2 Corinthians 1.22). 'What is to come', and is already at work among us, is the continual feast of resurrection life. To be a Christian means to be always young, in a sense far more profound than mere biological youthfulness. In the risen Christ, the Christian is always at the beginning of life. However far he progresses, he is always on the threshold of eternal life. By prayer the Christian has a resurrection stance in relation to life: he stands *at the start of life, before life;* in front of him are spread out the incredible riches 'guaranteed' to be his. 'All things are yours, whether . . . the world or life or death or the present or the future – all are yours, and you are of Christ, and Christ is of God' (1 Corinthians 3.21–2). Prayer is the language of Christian newness by which 'God's breath in man' goes one way, back to 'its birth'.

When we search through scripture for an event, or a personality, which reflects Christ's resurrection newness, we find David. The Philistine army fled before the audacious faith and courage of the boy with his sling. King Saul thought Goliath was too big to fight; David thought he was too big to miss. And there we have exemplified the weary cynicism of the cautious adult mind, and the uncompromising idealism and verve of youth. Even at his death Jesus was a young man. His vision, words and acts were never entirely at home within the disenchanted adult world. Irenaeus said about Jesus, 'Know that he brought all newness with him by bringing himself'.

His heart was bursting with the paradoxes of God's inventions, the exhilarating and subversive upside-down-ness of the kingdom: that we will find ourselves when we dare to throw ourselves away on to the will of God, and so on. The rigid, conformist, and above all the self-centred mind (the aging mind) cannot cope with him. His newness is spliced into this present sin-damaged time of ours and it is not an easy fit. Bernanos reflects Christ's young-ness with his comment: 'He who cannot give more than he receives is already starting to decay. Even a careless observer can see that a miser at twenty is already an old man.'[4] The biological aging process, which so terrifies our secular society, really is beside the point. Spiritual aging is far more destructive of the personality.

Jesus said on the secret of eternal young-ness, 'Do not store up for yourselves treasures on earth, where moth and rust destroy, and where thieves break in and steal. But store up for yourselves treasures in heaven, where moth and rust do not destroy, and where thieves do not break in and steal. For where your treasure is, there your heart will be also' (Matthew 6.19–21). Prayer as a way of life, a way of the heart, as 'God's breath in man returning to its birth', takes our essential life back and up, against the processes of 'moth and rust', into heaven and the inexhaustible, rejuvenating life of Christ.

In the spa resort of Ragatz in Switzerland you can walk into a mountain and, through a window in a door, look into a pool of steaming mineral water thrusting up from the depths. From that source water is drawn off into all the hotels, clinics, homes and drinking fountains. Paul said, 'If the Spirit of him who raised Jesus from the dead is living in you . . .' (Romans 8.11). Again, 'We have the mind of Christ' (1 Corinthians 2.16) in the Spirit who makes all things new. By prayer we are in communion with that mind which purges from our minds the silt and waste deposited by our natural 'old' cynicism. I witnessed this rejuvenating process in a congregation which, in obedience to the mind of Christ, had embarked upon a daring and costly church-planting project. It involved about one-third of the congregation moving out to start a new church. Exciting for those going into a new venture, while for those left behind it felt like a bereavement. But in the act of obeying the Lord, the spiritual life of the sending church lifted on to a new level. You could feel and touch the fresh life; 'the Spirit of him who raised Jesus from the dead is living in you'. They were growing younger. Needless to say that episode was immersed in prayer from beginning to end. Prayer in groups as well as privately, on Sundays, and in nights of prayer, to bring the mind of the church into the resurrection mind, the young, rejuvenating mind of Jesus by his Holy Spirit.

Bishop Basil said of the process, 'The person who reaches out for what lies ahead of him is always becoming younger than himself.'

CHAPTER 4

The soul in paraphrase, heart in pilgrimage

Another turn of the diamond, another image of prayer. How to unriddle 'The soul in paraphrase'? Begin with the part we understand: 'paraphrase' is a free rendering of a statement expressing its sense in different words. By analogy, your soul is your 'statement' to God and to the world; and prayer is the free rendering, the expansion and the amplification, of your soul-statement. But not everyone will greet this news with unbridled enthusiasm for fear that 'expansion' threatens serenity.

Our two earlier explorations of prayer as banqueting among angels, and as 'becoming younger than yourself', honoured the interior life. But talk of 'paraphrasing' suggests disruption and un-rooting. The soul as demolition site does not sit easily with inner calm.

A glance at the 'spirituality' section in the bookshops will confirm what we knew already by personal discovery, that prayer is used by many today as a way of survival, a defence against the uproar which for most people is daily life. There is, we feel, quite enough 'free rendering' going on out there already without throwing our soul-life into the mincing machine. Everything is up in the air, fast and superficial, thin, hollowed out. The old certainties are shaken to their roots, the traditional navigation beacons dimmed almost to extinction. Yet all is not lost while we have the inner room wherein to recover our sanity by reflection and prayer. It remains the one quiet place in a madhouse so please, please, don't turn it out of doors!

Hence the trend everywhere is towards meditative prayer and the healing sense of simply being before the Father without agendas and lists; like Hildegaard's 'feather upon the breath of God' or Hopkins' desire to be 'swayed about, mote-like in thy mighty glow'. Waiting hopefully because of the promise: 'Those who hope in the Lord will renew their strength. They will soar on wings like eagles; they will run and not grow weary, they will walk and not be faint' (Isaiah 40.31). Like the saints who 'cut themselves adrift as a will-less piece of wood on the high-seas of unfathomable love'.

Activists may scoff at 'the barricaded larder' (in the old days the food-store was kept padlocked for fear of marauding soldiers) as self-indulgent and escapist in the face of a needy world, but we know better. For without the refreshment, which comes from holy drifting, hopeful waiting, godly idleness, we will have nothing to bring to the world. Even as we ponder those images of resting in God we feel the stress seeping away from our minds. So, we must decide: to paraphrase or not to paraphrase?

The first thing to note is how in half-a-dozen words George Herbert gives the essence of Christian living as *movement*, with prayer in the engine room of that movement. Just as we cannot not breathe, so we cannot not move, and remain Christian. Static prayer is an absurdity, like a songbird afraid of heights. In the spiritual life standing still is already a going back for it refuses the reason for our existence, our high calling in Christ (Philippians 3.12–14). Augustine suggested that our perfection consists in knowing that we are not perfect: we are people still in the making as we walk on.

The Persian poet-mystic Jelaluddin Rumi (1207–73) likens personal resistance to 'paraphrase' to a reluctant embryo. It refuses to leave the womb because it will not believe the poet's assurance of a beautiful world outside. The poet reasons:

Little by little, wean yourself.

This is the gist of what I have to say.

From an embryo, whose nourishment comes in the blood,
move to an infant drinking milk,

to a child on solid food,
to a searcher after wisdom,
to a hunter of more invisible game.

Think how it is to have a conversation with an embryo.
You might say, 'The world outside is vast and intricate.
There are wheatfields and mountain passes,
    and orchards in bloom.

At night there are millions of galaxies, and in sunlight
the beauty of friends dancing at a wedding.'

You ask the embryo why he, or she, stays cooped up
in the dark with eyes closed.

                    Listen to the answer.

There is no 'other world.'
I only know what I've experienced.
You must be hallucinating.[1]

Before considering what 'paraphrasing the soul' means, first a comment about paraphrasing words, especially the words of prayers
printed in scripture. You will recall Herbert's opinion (see p. 3) that
the fruit of reading the Bible and listening to sermons and other
teaching occasions will appear in more effective praying. The best
way to read the psalms is to pray the psalms.

Scripture serves like a thriving maternity-ward, producing
prayers out of fertile mother-texts, that is, when our prayers come
to birth out of (paraphrased out of) scripture. Even those highly
personal, gasping cries recorded throughout the Gospels can be
freely rendered to express our own longings and fears. It is not
necessary to be out on rough water in an open boat to appropriate
the terrified shout, 'Save us, Lord; we are sinking' (Matthew 8.25).
Contexts other than waves and wind suit equally well: desperate
fears associated with marriage and family, work, health, accident,
depression, loneliness, etc. Similarly, we can take up Bartimaeus'

sob, 'I want my sight back' (Mark 10.51), or Peter's disillusioned 'Master, we were hard at work all night and caught nothing' (Luke 5.5). We hear it said all the time: 'I gave my best years to that job (– that marriage – that church) and look! It's come to nothing.' Cries waiting in scripture to be taken up, expanded and amplified into personal circumstances. Why else were those moments recorded if not for each generation's own urgent paraphrasing; their free rendering into the here-and-now moment?

When we do clothe our needs in biblical utterances it means we are not the first to do it. Somewhere in the ancient world a man or woman in a crisis coined a cry from the heart, which fits our own crisis. Also, when we submit our desire to pray to the prayers recorded in scripture under the Holy Spirit's direction, a nagging anxiety is resolved. 'We prayed but were we on the right wavelength? Were we getting through to God?' It is not possible to say yes or no to such subjective questionings other than with an equally subjective opinion: 'I felt it went well/not so well.' But when our prayers take their lead from scripture they become a response to a conversation already initiated and invited by the Holy Spirit. We can trust scripture to be 'on the right wavelength' and to be 'getting through' as the Spirit reaches out to us from his side by his inspired revelation.

In my own parish church last Sunday we were blessed with a fine instance of scripture-led praying. The person who led the intercessions (following the three scripture lessons) explained briefly that the prayers would be in response to the readings. He didn't use the word 'paraphrase' but that is what it was. Clearly he had pondered the readings beforehand and matched them to what he knew of the concerns of the congregation. Thus the scriptures, which were still ringing in our ears, were turned back to the Father carrying our prayers. It struck me as all so refreshingly simple and obvious. No impression here of someone indulging his pet whims, or prayers floating up out of a vague swarm of sentiments about life. These prayers were not clever or know-all-ish, nor that most appalling variety – perfect, flawless prayers which are also utterly safe, innocuous, toothless. Scripture and prayer illuminated each other in a quietly powerful manner. I felt – this is how to use scripture; and – this is how to pray. A young mother recently come to faith in Christ writes that it was the reality of prayer in her own church that convinced her. 'Our churches should reek of prayer . . . we should carry the scent of it on our clothes.' Yes, and scripture-inspired prayer has that incense quality.

Why cast around for things to pray for when the Holy Spirit has gone to such lengths in the inspiration and translations of scripture to give us prayers of the great pray-ers? When next you pray for your own congregation, or the wider Church, and wonder what to ask for on their behalf, consider the rich stock of paraphrasing available, for example, in Paul's seminal prayer for Christian people:

> For this reason I kneel before the Father, from whom his whole family in heaven and on earth derives its name. I pray that out of his glorious riches he may strengthen you with power through his Spirit in your inner being, so that Christ may dwell in your hearts through faith. And I pray that you, being rooted and established in love, may have power, together with all the saints, to grasp how wide and long and high and deep is the love of Christ, and to know this love that surpasses knowledge – that you may be filled to the measure of all the fullness of God. (Ephesians 3.14–19)

At least six theme-phrases await expansion and free rendering. Incidentally, it would not be an impossible task to memorize some of the prayers in scripture (a year, at one prayer a month, would accumulate a rich store). There is a world of difference between having a prayer on a page and having it 'by heart'. The Rabbis insisted, as a powerful incentive for memorizing scripture, 'What is known by heart, the heart knows.' Memorized, seminal model-prayers will keep us open to the Spirit's wavelength.

Our Lord's words will then apply also to the prayers in the heart: 'The good man brings good things out of the good stored up in his heart . . . For out of the overflow of his heart his mouth speaks' (Luke 6.45). There we have another word for paraphrase: 'overflow'.

(So much for our brief detour into paraphrasing prayers in

scripture.) But George Herbert speaks of prayer not as words in paraphrase but 'the soul' in paraphrase. What is this stuff called 'soul'?

The first thing to note is that we do not, none of us, have a soul. We *are* a soul, a 'living being' (Genesis 2.7). A surgeon probing inside a patient in search of the soul will have as much luck as a mechanic rummaging about inside the engine to find the car. A soul, a living being, is the result of God's creative, dynamic activity empowering man. The soul is 'man empowered by God'. It is 'person' or personality, the radical force of character. Soul is mind, but not in our usual restricted sense of the reasoning faculty only. The modern usage of 'mind' as the sphere of intellectual activity, separate from 'heart' as the place of feelings (usually warm, moving feelings), is quite alien to the biblical meaning of those terms.

Soul-mind includes everything that constitutes and colours the essence of a person: thought, felt-thought, emotion, perception, interest, and inclination. It is this essence which when paraphrased – expounded, amplified, extended in the overflow of a free rendering – becomes prayer: the essential self in all its powers and characteristics moving together as prayer. Including words, but words as one aspect of a total expression of personality. It may help to contrast it with an 'un-paraphrased' person who picks up prayer, uses it and puts it down again while he moves on to his next interest. Sweatless, controlled, he always keeps within his limits. His sincerity is not in question but when he prays only a part of himself is engaged.

We turn to our Lord Jesus for the definitive demonstration of prayer as the 'soul in paraphrase'. The first thing we notice about him is his complete integrity. He is what he prays. He stands fully, in all his powers, behind the words he utters. His prayers engage and express everything we understand by 'Jesus'. Consider his prayers from the cross: his prayer for the world while he was dying at the hands of the world and for the world. Austin Farrer comments, 'The prayer which saves the world is one with the existence of the man who prays.' With Jesus everything moves together in the same direction, will, emotion, intellect, decisions, action. Here is sublime paraphrasing, an expanding free rendering of his essence:

his body broken as bread, his blood poured out as wine for the life of the world. His cross is his prayer in the language of wood and iron.

With us it is sadly different for not everything moves together in the same direction. We are, at the best of times, a touch schizo-phrenic in our conflicting, contradictory desires. Yeats traced the confusion to:

> All that man is,
> All mere complexities
> The fury and the mire of human veins.
>
> ('Byzantium')

On the surface of the mind we utter our prayers, while beneath the surface our selfish energies and vanities move in their own very different directions.

Only one power can save by healing and reintegrating our torn interior life: love. And only the Holy Spirit of love can reach under the root of our being and there pour in his life and love into our hearts. 'We have . . . received . . . the Spirit who is from God, that we may understand what God has freely given us (1 Corinthians 2.12). But Urs von Balthasar's lovely comment will not allow us to use that verse as an easy cliché:

> To him [the Spirit] the most delicate, vulnerable, and precious one in God, we must open ourselves up, without defensiveness, without thinking that we know better, without hardening our-selves, so that we may undergo initiation by him into the mystery that God is love. Let us not imagine that we already know this ourselves! 'In this is love, not that we loved God, but that he loved us and sent his son to be the expiation of our sins' (1 John 4.10). The Spirit alone teaches us this reversal of perspective, but through him we can really learn what, in his view, love is.[2]

Love insists that prayer become 'the soul in paraphrase'. Love will articulate her concerns through our personal powers expanding, amplifying and free-rendering out to people. Love takes people seriously and requires that we share that seriousness by observing and reading them appropriately. Auden said, 'The only quality which all human beings without exception possess is uniqueness.' Love is fascinated by people and longs to know more about them in their unique particularity.

Lazy, slapdash praying cannot be bothered to 'see' people. Our fundamental attitude towards others determines whether or not we are able to see the people we pray for. The great photojournalist Gisele Freund said about photography, 'When you do not like human beings, you cannot make good portraits.' Her personal warmth, humanity and gifts of friendship seemed to affect what went on inside her camera and the outcome of her photography! Something similar could be said about prayer. We could usefully write over our prayer-lists: 'Am I serious about these people? Am I sincere? Have I tried to "see" this person with a generous eye? Is "my soul in paraphrase" here or am I just going through the motions and reeling off names?'

Prayer is the outflowing of our powers of observation, intuition, and perception at the disposal of love. The use of the tongue in spoken prayer has its part at the end of our investigative activity. If this sounds altogether far too demanding (it is in fact a way of life) remember, we are the children of a shepherd who left the 99 in order to seek out the one, who in his ministry, and with such limited time available to him, spent (or so it seems to us) a dispro-portionate amount of it on the ones and twos.

It does take time to 'see' a person. An individual's personal depth is drawn in part from the subtle and complex web of relationships within which she lives and by which she is defined and formed. Jesus became the man he was, humanly speaking, because his parents and family, neighbours, friends, Rabbi, etc. were who they were in Nazareth. To pray in any depth for someone requires some interest in their formation and that we pray for them along the pathways of their web of relationships. As with so much else in the Christian life the principle in our praying should be 'stop counting, start weighing'. Never mind the width, feel the texture of your prayer.

There is a touch of the Sherlock Holmes about 'soul in paraphrase' prayer. He of course was the supreme observer and interpreter of human behaviour at a time when the new manufacturing processes were knocking individuality and eccentricity out of people. Holmes revelled in the odd particularity of people, and the masses loved him for it. He searched for the unique story which he, like Auden, assumed was encoded in each person's life. Everything mattered – a scratch, a way of sitting, a way of pronouncing a certain vowel, a scuff on a shoe. Together they were signs differentiating this person from the rest. For people affected by the conforming pressures of the work place, it was intoxicating to be told by the great man that they carried within them a unique narrative. Holmes observed people in order to solve their mysteries; we will do it out of respect and in order to pray for them. Through prayer as 'the soul in paraphrase' we face out towards others, we will want to know about them in order to pray for them. We are in that sense lending ourselves to others. Something extraordinary and mysterious happens in return – we receive ourselves back from 'paraphrasing' enriched and expanded. We actualize ourselves (not by deliberate intention but as a result) in loving and praying for others. Jesus said: 'Give, and it will be given to you . . . For with the measure you use, it will be measured to you' (Luke 6.38).

*Prayer is also 'the **heart in pilgrimage**'.*

The heart, like the soul, is not a 'thing' as in popular imagining. It is 'the soul as an operating force'. The heart is the soul, the living being, the person, in action. The state of the heart in biblical usage dominates every manifestation of life (Proverbs 14.30; 15.13; 17.22) – health, courage, fear, mood, temperament, wishing, reasoning, reflecting, considering, insight. It is the treasury of knowledge and memory, will and decision. In contradiction of our customary use of the term, the heart in biblical understanding least of all means the emotions! On the contrary, it much more frequently means the organ of knowledge, with which is associated the will and its plans and intentions, one's consciousness. When *this* heart is in pilgrimage, prayer happens.

The heart carries within it a feeling of something like homesickness. A sense of unease and impermanence in this world; fragments of a haunting memory of an enchanting place to which we belong.

It is as though the Father sends a signal from out of eternity to his children in this world; we lock on to it and follow it home. A helpful analogy is *syntonization*. The sounding of a note on one instrument produces the corresponding note on another instrument, or as if a child hums and dances as she listens to a tune playing. The higher energy of love (God's own energy) is communicated, and an essentially inferior energy (our own) starts repeating the rhythm of the superior one in its own fashion. As when a stick thrown into a swirling stream takes on the motion of the stream, or a rider on horseback sways to the movement of the horse.

Therefore our most vital spiritual preparation each day will be to attune our hearts to the Father's incoming rhythms. Nothing else comes close in importance. Look at von Balthasar's comment once again, that 'we must open ourselves up to the Spirit' (p. 31). Syntonization occurs in the Holy Spirit's moving between the Father's heart and our own.

Notice that Herbert is not saying the obvious thing here, that the heart prays as it journeys, though of course it does. Or that we pray for our heart to make a good pilgrimage, though of course we do. But Herbert is saying the pilgrimage *is* the prayer of the heart: prayer is 'the heart in pilgrimage'. Prayer is not, as we are prone to think, one aspect of the pilgrimage along with numerous others. The act of a life walking through the world to the Father, step-by-step and day-by-day in Christian obedience, constitutes prayer. Everything in this journeying is the prayer. Once again we encounter Herbert's ability to reconcile and heal the deeply felt split in our minds between the sacred and the secular. Everything in our lives is drawn into the walk, breathing its praise and prayer to the Father with every step taken.

Noah provides a striking example of the sacredness of the secular when rendered up to God. Noah 'walked with God' (Genesis 6.9), but if that phrase conjures a picture of an unearthly mystic tapped into secret sources of spiritual power, we should remember 'the Rabbis insist that *doing* a commandment of God is an act of communion with him' (G. A. F. Knight). In the act of cutting wood, in hammering nails, and with every lick of paint for the ark, Noah was walking with God: his boat-building was the prayer. Receive the work before you this day, *all* work not just 'religious' acts (that split again!), as your pilgrimage, and let your whole-hearted completion of the work be your prayer.

A last thought on the practice of pilgrimage in the England of Herbert's time. There was of course much excessive interest in seeking out the holy as concretely embodied in sacred places, a practice, writes Eamon Duffy, '[o]ften criticized in the late Middle Ages, not least by Thomas à Kempis in the *Imitation of Christ*'. (The Reformers were not first to address the problem!)

But discerning, spiritually minded Christians valued pilgrimage for its more important symbolic and integrative functions, helping the believer to place the religious routine of the closed and concrete worlds of household, parish, or guild in a broader and more complex perception of the sacred, which transcends while affirming local allegiances.[3] Pilgrimage broadens the mind! We could even say it expands and amplifies the pilgrim in a free rendering of his life. The heart in pilgrimage is a case of 'the soul in paraphrase'.

CHAPTER 5

The Christian plummet sounding heaven and earth

A small warning light flashed in the margin of page 25. If you noticed it, congratulations. If not, take care, for it was signalling something important. There we were talking about our use of prayer as a balm for jangled nerves and the unquiet heart. But lurking around the edges of that perfectly reasonable view of prayer (and here is where we need the warning lights and alarm bells) is the attractive fallacy that the real business of prayer is with my business. Not in theory, or in public, for what Christian wouldn't sign up to prayer for the big needs of the wider world? But in practice, and with no more effort than it takes to just go with the flow of my self-centred inclinations, when it comes to praying 'happiness is a small circle': my small tight circle of immediate concerns, my family and a few friends. Our sympathies escape the pull of the small circle only with great difficulty, and then only if they come under the sway of a new, wholly superior dynamic. Hence the timeliness of this latest metaphor. The challenge in this exploration will be to bring our present vision of prayer, its range and scope, to be scrutinized by the unusual idea of prayer as 'the Christian plummet sounding heaven and earth'.

Imagine you are located at the mid-point between heaven and earth. You are hang-gliding there, perhaps, or magically floating. In your hand you have the gift of prayer in the shape of a plummet, a plumb-line, the sort sailors in small boats use to 'sound' the depth of water under the keel. Your plumb-line/prayer-line possesses several unusual properties: first, it can go vertically up, lead first, to sound height, as well as in the more usual direction, down, to gauge depth. Second, its string is limitless in length. And third, it is a thinking plummet. Just let it go, down or up, into any subject and it will run and run to the farthest limits. It is a 'getting-to-the-bottom-of-things' plummet.

By this picture George Herbert suggests the real business of prayer: penetration into the heart and essence of things, into origins and root-causes of whatever prayer is concerned with; like a friend who, if you mention a headache, or lack of money, will not leave it there but wants to know the full story in order to help. 'Sounding-prayer' is quite incapable of being superficial. It isn't in its nature to deal with the outside of things. It transcends, or transfixes, the merely material and visible, touchable world to reach into its centre where the outcomes are decided. Thus, when praying for God's blessing on people sounding-prayer bucks the prevailing fashions. It penetrates beyond the current myths of the-latest-is-the-greatest, and, the-newer-is-the-truer. It calls the bluff of the obvious, the mere appearance of things as perceived by the natural eye alone, those masks which would deflect enquiry into the true source of things within. Sounding-prayer remains unimpressed by the posturings of our boring, one-dimensional, consumerist culture. It probes and pries and asks, 'What drives this show?'

In the spectrum of prayer, at one end are those kindly but vague 'Dear Lord, please bless everyone everywhere' sort of requests. At the other end are prayers like a 'plummet sounding heaven and earth'. Take, for example, the great clamouring issue of our time, 'personal freedom', and the rights of the individual to make significant life-directing choices. We may simply bring the matter to God with 'please grant personal freedom to the peoples of the world'. What could be more safely Christian? Individual freedom of choice is a very good thing, which everyone should enjoy. But 'sounding-prayer' people, with their instinct for getting to the heart of things, suspect that there may be more than meets the eye in this issue. For one thing, it is not without significance that the vast advertising industry appears terribly interested in the subject. Indeed 'choice' is market language, and 'individual freedom of choice' is milked as a potent fashion statement.

It seems that it doesn't matter greatly what, or who, or how you choose just as long as you have plenty of options, for that is your 'human right'. One hair-raising definition of what it means to be a human being runs, 'The essence of our nature is freedom to re-define ourselves', which introduces all manner of complexities. A recent survey in North America reveals disturbing side effects of 'freedom of individual choice' when pursued relentlessly and mercilessly. Thirty per cent of all pregnancies are terminated; i.e., one person's freedom to choose results directly in another's total and final negation. Thirty per cent of children born are welcomed into the world by one parent only. The father has chosen not to stay, presumably in exercise of his inalienable right to 'be true to himself' in seeking the lifestyle best for himself. That individual's freedom of choice results directly in the outright rejection of his child. Thirty per cent of children born into a family with both parents will see them divorced by the age of ten. In summary, a culture built upon the unquestioned supremacy of individual choice is creating a monstrous twin culture of massive rejection of children. The consequences piling up for society in the years ahead stagger the imagination.

Such evidence is fuel for intelligent prayer, which sounds the depths of society. Personal freedom is an *essential tool* for living the good life. To be able to love and serve another, be it God or my neighbour, requires the freedom to choose to do so.

At the same time we will pray against those very powerful and apparently irresistible tendencies in society that celebrate personal freedom as a god-like thing and an end in itself. That way ends in the prevailing culture of death: abuse, violence, self-destructiveness, promiscuity and divorce, bizarre sexual excesses, damaged children, fear of the dark, runaway greed, disease and so forth. In a word, the contents of your newspaper on an average day. We will pray not merely for 'personal freedoms' but for the recovery of wisdom in the life of our societies, a right grasp on reality as a way of building a counter-culture of life against the culture of death.

What does prayer discover when it 'sounds heaven and earth'? Jesus' own ministry was itself a visitation (a plummeting) of every inch and ounce of the created order, spiritual and physical: 'When he ascended on high . . . What does "he ascended" mean except that he also descended to the lower, earthly regions? He who descended is the very one who ascended higher than all the heavens, in order to fill the whole universe' (Ephesians 4.8–10). Christ *is* the prayer sounding heaven and earth. At their very best and most penetrative, our prayers merely ride on his. He emerged with his findings, which he presents in the form of 'The Lord's Prayer'. All that the world yearns for in her deepest heart, is answered by all that heaven longs to bestow of herself.

- Heaven is not a place but a relationship. It is where God dwells.
- Heaven is where the Father is adored as creation's high king, his name hallowed, his will the delight of his people.
- Earth is created and gifted to answer heaven, to mirror back the holy love and joy of heaven: 'on earth as it is in heaven' (Matthew 6.9, 10).
- Within that context, the Father reckons our daily necessities as much his concern as his cosmic plans (Matthew 6.11–13).

'On earth as it is in heaven' amounts to nothing less than God's practical reign among us. Whatever particular matter engages our prayer, and however we frame our petitions, we are asking for the Lord to hold sway in that situation. We can ask for nothing greater, we are not permitted to ask for anything less. Jesus said, 'This, then, is how you should pray...'

Certain questions and some un-certainties arise in our minds as we attempt sounding-prayer. Most urgently we require clarification concerning 'the kingdom of God'. What is it? Would you recognize it if you met it in the street? Social programmes of all stripes have annexed the term. What did Jesus mean by it?

He launched his mission, 'proclaiming the good news of God. "The time has come," he said. "The kingdom of God is near. Repent and believe the good news!"'(Mark 1.14–15)

If we are to pray realistically and with conviction for the kingdom to come among us, how can we reconcile Jesus' claims with the depressing reality of much in the world? It doesn't *look* as though the kingdom has 'come near'.

C. E. B. Cranfield comments that 'the kingdom has come and is still to come because Jesus has come and is to come'. He came, but 'none of the rulers of this age understood it, for if they had, they would not have crucified the Lord of glory' (1 Corinthians 2.8). He came but his glory was hidden; the kingdom came in him but it was a 'veiled manifestation'. In his incarnation he won the victory for the kingdom, a final and absolute victory; nothing else remains to be done. 'It is finished' (John 19.30). But in this present age it is concealed from the eyes and minds of the world. He brought the kingdom but not in an incontrovertible manner that would leave people with no choice but to accept, like it or not. Christ is truly Lord and King, not a virtual or symbolic one.

It is more helpful to understand his reign not as moving from little to much, from partial to complete, but from veiled to manifest, from hidden to revealed. The kingdom in all its fulness came in Christ since he himself came fully. 'For God was pleased to have all his fulness dwell in him' (Colossians 1.19). When we pray 'Your kingdom come' we are not asking for something more powerful or complete to happen, but for that which is already complete to be seen in its (i.e., in Christ's) true glory; for the incognito to be removed and for the king to be known for who he is.

Our hope does not move from less to more. The kingdom does not follow the curve of progress and development with incremental gains, step-by-step and inch-by-inch (which can, as we know only too well, also be *reversed*). We pray for what is already fully there to stand forth and be seen. Our hope will move from faith to sight; from one moment to the next. What has been 'there' all the time may suddenly be seen for what it is. The screens and curtains are momentarily pulled back to reveal the truth (i.e., the Christ) but closed again until that time known only to the Father, when all screens and barriers are removed for ever and the Lord Jesus Christ adored by all creation.

Therefore sounding-prayers, which reach to the heart and essence of heaven and earth, must go behind the screens of the senses to see by faith what is the truth of things. The Book of Revelation goes behind visible history to tell the story from the perspective of the kingdom of God. 'Revelation' is world theatre; the unveiling of Jesus Christ as Lord of history and of current events. The visible story as experienced by Christians living under the Roman Imperial authority in first-century Asia Minor was bleak. Persecution and the real possibility of cruel martyrdom were boiling up over the heads of the young churches. Yet every Lord's Day they went to celebrate the fact that Jesus is Lord over all, including Caesar. Would their vision of Jesus be exalted and compelling enough to keep them faithful to him regardless of the consequences? Remember, a simple action like a pinch of incense into the flame at Caesar's shrine could save a Christian. Sincerity was not required! The series of visions, which is the Book of Revelation, was given through John to convince the churches where the truth lay. It took them, and it takes us today, behind the scenes. Nothing could more strengthen and excite our prayer-life, as well as increasing its scope and range, than meditation in the visions of 'the throne' in Revelation chapters 4 and 5. Here are a few points by way of guidance into those sections.

Chapter 4 is about attaining critical height. Left to ourselves, embedded as we are in the present moment, we are unable to see over and around, and all sides of, the truth. We are like a man standing so close to a brick wall that he cannot say if the building is a cathedral or a bus shelter. We must have some critical distance from, and height above, the present order in order to see what is going on. We follow John through a trap door into heaven (4.1) and find ourselves standing in what appears to be part temple and part military command centre at 'Supreme HQ'. Around us move signs, symbols, people, creatures, and lights. They are apocalyptic indicators of the scope of the conflict, taking place on earth between heaven and hell. Over everything and dominating the entire scene is the throne of God (v. 2), indicating that whatever the ebb and flow of the warfare, its outcome is already decided. This is a genuine battle with real consequences for real winners and real losers, but from first to last the divine sovereignty dominates. We view everything from this vantage point of the throne of God; that is from the perspective of the kingdom of Christ.

The vision is expanded in chapter 5 and provides further inspiration for our prayers. God upon the throne holds in his right hand a scroll covered in writing (the divine plan for mankind). Fine, so there *is* a mind at work behind the ways of the world and its history! The crisis is created by the fact that the good and perfect will of God is written in the scroll but the scroll is 'sealed with seven seals' which in Revelation code signifies completely, fully, perfectly sealed up. This will-of-God-scroll is not releasing its wisdom and grace into the world. The angelic onlookers are appalled at the implication of a closed scroll. If the will of God is not running through the affairs of the world in a controlling and shaping fashion, then whose will is it at work?

The implication is that the demonic powers will rush in to fill the vacuum. The cry goes out for someone 'worthy to break the seals and open the scroll' but 'no-one in heaven or on earth or under the earth could open the scroll or even look inside it' (5.2, 3). The call has echoed throughout history, and the heavenlies, for someone qualified to take the scroll and open it. Then John in his vision sees a person (actually he says, 'I saw a Lamb'), and we are left in no doubt about his identity for it was 'looking as if it had been slain' (v. 6). Jesus Christ has won the right, by his atoning death on the cross, to take and to open the scroll. All heaven erupts in doxology: 'Worthy is the Lamb, who was slain, to receive power and wealth and wisdom and strength and honour and glory and praise!' (v. 12).

The stunning throne-vision compels our prayer, up and out, in intercession for the peoples of the world. The extraordinary upheavals and movements of peoples around the globe are as much news of God as they are world news. The scroll in the hand of the One on the throne is open and streaming into the life-blood of the nations. God is not their puppeteer. He allows the nations their freedom while drawing all things to serve his purposes. 'The nations' are the theatre of his activity and a vehicle of his purposes. Grasping the significance of this, we attend to world news more carefully and prayerfully; we become habitual world-watchers, more global-minded. 'Reading the morning papers becomes a religious act, for it sets the agenda of what must be repaired this day' (Kushner). But if world affairs are not significant in our thinking and praying (nor reflected in our church programmes) we imply an empty throne or a sealed scroll, an absentee or powerless God, or that 'salvation' is essentially a disembodied 'spiritual' programme floating clear of the messy rough and tumble of 'the nations'. In which case we are back in the 'happiness is a small circle' fallacy.

But sounding-prayer will, by its nature and by its dynamic connection with 'the throne' of the Revelation visions, make us cosmic people.

CHAPTER 6

Engine against the Almighty, sinner's tower

We pray because prayer works. We wouldn't if it didn't; and we certainly wouldn't spend time meditating on an old prayer-sonnet. Prayer works, not on account of any excellence in our practice of prayer, but because, and only because, we pray in the name of Jesus. At one with him, his Holy Spirit attuning our mind and prayer to his, what we ask is what he asks. Our asking is taken into and participates in his asking. What Christ asks is asked by God from God, by God the Son from God the Father who cannot refuse the Son.

Just how God answers our prayers, the manner and the timing, is a mystery we leave among 'the secret things which belong to the Lord our God' (Deuteronomy 29.29). The fact that we are not able to trace the path of God's response does not affect our praying one little bit. A child doesn't wait until she understands the chemistry of oxygen or the physiology of the lungs before she breathes. We celebrate the fact that God's ways and means of answering prayer elude our grasp for his repertoire of action is as limitless as his imagination. Austin Farrer says about that range of action, 'His plans for us are what perfect wisdom suggest to infinite love; his plans for us are his love, they are all the good that his love can see for us.'[1] Can you keep track of his infinite love? No more can we his ways of answering our prayers.

We pray because prayer works, and because it changes things. It changes the world and it is able to penetrate the hearts of men to change their ways. According to this latest facet of Herbert's diamond, prayer even 'changes' God, in the sense that a captor 'changes' his prisoner. This hair-raising, staggeringly risky picture takes up the idea of the old military engineer's construction for siege and assault, his 'engine' to batter the enemy's defences, tunnel under his trenches and blow open the gates of his fortress. We might wonder how such a violent image could commend itself to Herbert's sensitive, peaceable, artistic mind. Perhaps we need look no further than to a famous friend of the Herbert family.

John Donne – poet, soldier, great preacher – had a dramatic and bloody introduction to warfare when serving with an English force that surprised and destroyed a Spanish fleet in Cadiz harbour in 1597. They captured and razed the city, its castle and its fortifications. Did Donne fill the young George Herbert's head with stories of 'engines against the Spanish'? Herbert coined a nice image from naval warfare:

> Love's a man-of-war,
> And can shoot,
> And can hit from far.
> ('Discipline')

Donne himself used assault-language to implore God to come and do something drastic about his state of life:

> Batter my heart, three-personed God; for, you
> As yet but knock, breathe, shine, and seek to mend;
> That I may rise, and stand, o'erthrow me, and bend
> Your force, to break, blow, burn and make me new.
> ('Divine Meditations' 14)

Spiritual violence directed towards personal sanctification, we can understand. Who of us wouldn't use Donne's plea for ourselves? Also we can understand prayer as an essential weapon in spiritual warfare 'against the powers of this dark world and against the spiritual forces of evil in the heavenly realms. Therefore . . . pray in the Spirit on all occasions with all kinds of prayers and requests' (Ephesians 6.12, 18). But Herbert is suggesting something quite different when he turns the assault-engine against the Lord himself!

There is a high 'cringe-factor' in this sort of thinking. It smacks of over-familiarity with the holiest things, an irreverence that feels half-blasphemous. Like the person who delights to announce, with a knowing chuckle, 'When I get to heaven I'm going to give the Lord a piece of my mind. He's got some explaining to do over what happened to the weather on the Sunday school outing!' What is intended to imply a confident, man-to-man, chummy relationship with the Almighty merely comes across as excruciatingly banal and irreverent.

But we are thinking here of Donne and Herbert's insights into the way of prayer, not some pompous pip-squeak in the next parish. We can teach those seventeenth-century believers nothing about reverential love for God. They reveal by their writings an enviable balance in their vision of life in Christ. Fully assured of salvation by the blood of Christ and of his unbreakable friendship, at the same time they kept a healthy and realistic awareness of their frailty, of life hanging by a thread. Herbert writes:

> Only my soul hangs on thy promises
> With face and hands clinging unto thy breast,
> Clinging and crying, crying without cease,
> Thou art my rock, thou art my rest.
>
> ('Perseverance')

No trace here of over-familiarity with the Lord. It suggests rather a mountaineer pressed up against a rock-face, holding on, just, by the tips of his fingers.

Donne's 'Hymn to God the Father' is another beautiful and deeply moving expression of reverential 'finger-tips' dependence upon Christ for a safe passage through death and judgement:

> Wilt thou forgive that sin where I begun,
> Which was my sin, though it were done before?
> Wilt thou forgive that sin, through which I run,
> And do run still: though still I do deplore?
> When thou hast done, thou hast not done,
> For, I have more.

Engine against the Almighty, sinner's tower

Wilt thou forgive that sin which I have won
   Others to sin? and, made my sin their door?
Wilt thou forgive that sin which I did shun
   A year, or two: but wallowed in, a score?
     When thou hast done, thou hast not done,
      For I have more.

I have a sin of fear, that when I have spun
   My last thread, I shall perish on the shore;
But swear by thy self, that at my death thy son
   Shall shine as he shines now, and heretofore;
     And, having done that, thou hast done,
      I fear no more.

Those examples may serve to answer fears that the idea of prayer as an 'engine against the Almighty' is the product of an overheated fanatical imagination, or a flippant mind. Donne and Herbert reverenced God as the One upon the throne before whose holiness 'earth and sky fled from his presence' (Revelation 20.11). Paradoxically, the infinite freedom and almighty power of God reveal themselves most not in acts of irresistible might, but by his voluntary self-limiting which invites and makes room for us to enter into the 'prayer-engine' game with him.

If this is not a too trivial illustration of our 'prayer-engine' relationship with God, our small granddaughter has been staying with us for a few days. Initially (and this period of time is rapidly growing shorter and shorter with each visit!) there was the usual shyness as she quietly checked out the house and the lie of the land. Then, as her self-confidence and sense of being at home with us increased, a delightful change occurred. Our games together soon moved from granddad showing granddaughter how to play, to granddad and granddaughter playing as equals, to granddaughter taking the show over, creatively modifying the rules (in my day this was called cheating), throwing her weight about, running circles around the old man, drenching him with the garden hose (and being drenched in return), shrieking with laughter at the mayhem, and generally bossing granddad into near exhaustion. What is this child's 'engine against grandparents'? Her certainty of her secure place within our love for her and our pleasure in her confidence.

Jesus said that 'anyone who will not receive the kingdom of God like a little child will never enter it' (Luke 18.17); he or she will also never have the confidence to dare to use prayer as an 'engine against the Almighty'. Once again George MacDonald's great aphorism comes to mind, that 'it is the heart that is not yet sure of its God that is afraid to laugh in his presence'. The Church has always practised this aspect of prayer ministry, especially when up against it. Perhaps it is not surprising that the more comfortable and at ease we are in life, in material terms, the more the urgency drains away from our use of prayer. Bishop Eliud from the Diocese of Bungoma in Kenya said, on a recent visit to this country, that the key to growth of the Church in his country is prayer and self-giving. 'If you visit Bungoma, one thing you will soon get bored with is prayer! We pray at all times and in all places. When someone gets sick, for example, we may have no transport to get them to hospital. The only weapon we have is prayer.' Prayer as condoned violence directed at heaven and against God with his full permission. John Donne again:

> Earnest prayer has the nature of importunity... We press, we importune God... prayer has the nature of impudence; we threaten God in prayer... and God suffers this impudence and more. Prayer has the nature of violence; in the public prayers of the congregation, we besiege God, says Tertullian, and we take God prisoner, and bring God to our conditions, and God is glad to be straitened by us in that siege.[2]

Any reluctance on our part to take up the offer of engine-prayer may not, after all, be a sign of our high-minded concern for the dignity of God's honour. Rather it may be due more to our inability 'to laugh in his presence' or to accept that he could possibly give himself away to us and lay himself open so 'foolishly'. But surely the cross has settled that question for all time.

Prayer as 'engine against the Almighty' is supported by examples from throughout scripture. We will settle for one, the great seminal episode, which is the origin and source of the belief that heaven and

God welcome our onslaught in prayer: Jacob at the river Jabbok (Genesis 32.22–32).

If ever a man needed divine intervention it was Jacob at that moment. His brother, Esau, the one he famously swindled out of his inheritance, was on his way to find him with four hundred men, doubtless determined to settle an old score. Not surprisingly, Jacob was 'in great fear and distress' (v. 7), alone and waiting for Esau to catch up with him. But he had God's promise, given in the ladder-dream at Bethel (28.1–19), a reaffirmation of the ancient and unconditional covenant promise made to Abraham and his descendants, chosen to carry forward the covenant on behalf of the world: 'I am with you and will watch over you wherever you go . . . I will not leave you until I have done what I have promised you' (28.15). How a man in a tight corner can put that promise to work is unforgettably demonstrated in what happened next.

This was the moment, if ever there was one, for God to come through with his promised protection and blessing. How do you picture to yourself God's blessing coming into your life? Like an empty container waiting to be filled, perhaps, or a parched garden watered by a downpour of rain. But in this moment, when Jacob and his future nation receive their new name of 'Israel', God invites him to wrestle for his blessing. 'So Jacob was left alone, and a man wrestled with him till daybreak' (32.24). We know 'the man' was a theophany, God incognito, for next day Jacob named the place Peniel, meaning 'I saw God face to face' and lived to tell his story.

What passed through Jacob's mind as he grappled with his opponent, crashing around on the bank and in the river? At some point the realization dawned (or was it a lightning flash of revelation?) that he was fighting with a God-man, a man representing God: God-as-this-man. Instead of the textbook orthodox reaction – leaping back as if he had touched ten thousand volts, or falling flat on his face in abject submission – he seized the moment to claim full payment on the promises. What had been given in words – heard in the head, mediated through intellectual processes, carried in the memory – is now incarnated; the promise is here in flesh and blood gasping, panting and in his grip. Now he will hold God, literally, to his word. No question here of theological subtleties,

God had fallen into his embrace and Jacob will not let him go: sweat, pain, exertion, until he had wrestled God to the ground. Queensberry rules do not apply here where a man holds God to his word. When the man-God pleads for an end to the match Jacob responds with an even stronger hold.

Here is the paradoxical logic of prayer as an 'engine against the Almighty'. Only God can bless, but he allows himself to be overwhelmed and taken. 'I will not let you go unless you bless me.' Is there an element here of God testing out our quality: the quality of our seriousness and single-mindedness in our relationship with him? Questions such as 'Do we mean business?' 'How much do we value and desire God's life in our lives?' cannot be answered without testing and struggle which expose our sincerity and commitment. There is such a thing as casting pearls before swine. God's promises and his gracious invitations, if left untested on the pages of scripture, or in the memory, have no hands and feet or indeed no embodiment at all. Our spiritual life then drifts into the theoretical, unreal form of unproven knowledge.

Jacob's strange encounter prefigures the word of God taking flesh, to become immediate and tangible; graspable: 'that which was from the beginning, which we have heard, which we have seen with our eyes, which we have looked at and our hands have touched' (1 John 1.1). Which is to say, that in Christ God put himself within our grasp as he had put himself within Jacob's grasp on that mysterious occasion. Jacob wrestled his opponent into submission in that tough, rough, desperate, physical fight because God had set it up that way. At some point Jacob said to himself, 'O my God! It's God!! I don't know what's going on here but now I have him I'll show him how desperately I need him for myself, my family, and my future people. If this is God, I'll prove to him that I believe him with every scrap of energy within me. Everything I have known about God – those amazing stories, the traditions, the prayers, the history (all words, words, words) are now in my embrace and I will not let go until I have the blessing' – something along those lines?

In other words, by allowing prayer to become an 'engine against the Almighty' God is saying to us 'I mean it – do you mean it?' It has nothing to do with blackmailing God by setting up a clamour. Jesus teaches that we best bear witness to God as the Father of love precisely by the brevity and simplicity of our prayers: 'When you pray, do not keep on babbling like pagans, for they think they will be heard because of their many words' (Matthew 6.7). Not in the saying of words, or even in the words we say, so much as the heart dead-set on taking God's promises seriously, simply, immediately, at face value, and turning them back to him.

Notice two effects of Jacob's encounter. First, he carried the evidence of it in the way he walked. God's sly humour? Was this a tongue-in-cheek wrestling match? Jacob wins but walks for the rest of his days with a limp, to help him keep his 'victory' in perspective. *A limping people who overcome God in prayer* – not a bad description of a vital church. Second, the name-changing. No longer Jacob ('deceiver') but Israel (Genesis 32.28). Notice that the new name of Israel, says von Rad, 'is here interpreted very freely and contrary to its original meaning ("may God rule") in such a way that God is not the subject ("he rules") but the object ("he is ruled").' Could God have chosen a more unambiguous way to indicate his pleasure at Jacob's tenacious, tough-minded, audacious faith? The new name tells the world – this man wrestled with God and over-came. The limp tells the world – look at the weakness of this man's strength.

And prayer is a tower as well as an engine: a *'sinner's tower'*.

What can Herbert mean? Which tower? When a person whose imagination is soaked in scripture speaks of a tower, my guess is he has in mind *the* tower, the one at Babel (Genesis 11). But that construction was anything but a sinner's tower, in the sense that it was built by people who were humbly and realistically conscious of their sin before God. Rather the reverse, for in the eyes of its builders at Babel, it was a superb tower worthy of a wondrous city (Babel also means 'Gate of God'). An entrepreneur's tower, a tower for a triumphant empire-building people, a fitting symbol of a progressive people's self-sufficiency, a technocrat's tower, an edifice for a can-do society. With all the benefits of urban technology, frankly who needs to take God seriously? So runs the myth of Babel, Nineveh, Rome, New York and the megalopolis of our own era. 'It is only in an urban civilization that man has the metaphysical possibility of saying "I killed God"'.[3] Or if not killed exactly, harnessed and set to work, for God has his uses in the city. He can be placed on top of our brilliant tower that connects the city to heaven, and from there exercise a chaplaincy role. He rubber-stamps our plans and sanctions our schemes, bestowing a spiritual glow on our thoroughgoing secularism.

Babel is a religious tower. It was a people's expression of their spiritual aspirations, a people whose faith was in their power to think and build up to God, which is religion. But sinners know it to be a futile exercise; we place our faith in the tower of revelation, which God builds from heaven down to earth. The Babel tower had a central mediatorial role in connecting mankind to heaven. In the 'sinner's tower' Christ is the one, all-sufficient mediator between God and men. Prayer is that 'tower', it is our voice carried to God on Christ's voice, our expression gathered into his and offered to the Father as his. The sinner's tower is that *there is no tower*! There is only Christ, our unbreakable connection with the Father. All else is mere religion. Therefore we say as the justification of our prayers: 'We ask all these things in Jesus' name. Amen.'

CHAPTER 7

Reversed thunder,
Christ-side-piercing spear

Two wild pictures of prayer charged with an intensity of wisdom and with a whiff of anarchy. Prayer is God-sponsored subversion. Nothing is safe from its penetration; no power structure, tyrant or demon is free from its interference. 'Satan has asked to sift you as wheat. But I have prayed for you' (Luke 22.31–2). Prayer inverts pecking orders, the who's who and what's what. Not because it strives to be controversial or Bolshie, an angry voice shouting abuse from the touchlines, but because it surveys the action from alongside the throne of God. Prayer has its distinctive and revolutionary stance, even daring to turn God's own war-engine against him as it lays siege to heaven. Prayer is the great iconoclast, scorning man's high-prestige earth-to-heaven communications tower at Babel, rebuilding it from heaven to earth at Pentecost. Prayer reverses things, even thunder. Prayer is 'reversed thunder'.

This is a startling idea (made up of two non-startling words – but that's poetry for you!) even for Herbert's imagination. Do you wish to explore further into the potency and aggression of prayer? Contemplate thunder!

If only we could. We are quite unable to whistle up even a small thunderstorm as an audio-aid for our reflection. Always we are on the receiving end of the stuff, we are thundered at, and upon, when and wherever it is pleased to perform. We have no command or control over it, which is a humbling thought for children of a technically masterful culture. Herbert's diamond is flashing the suggestion that what thunder does to us on earth, our prayers do to God in his heaven; prayer, like thunder, cannot be withstood. In Jesus' estimation to be equipped with prayer is enough, that and the

Holy Spirit, or more exactly prayer *in* the Holy Spirit. Our Lord left us with little else in this world other than, 'I tell you the truth, my Father will give you whatever you ask in my name . . . Ask and you will receive, and your joy will be complete' (John 16.23, 24).

You have discovered, in our meditations so far in this book, that the way to enter Herbert's images is to pray them. His ideas, which can appear elusive, teasing and exotic on paper, yield power and illumination when we cease trying to 'solve' them and instead act upon them in prayer; use them as if they were true in prayer, and thus allow them room to prove their wisdom to us.

Thunder explodes, rattling the teacups, loosening slates on the roof, terrifying small children and large dogs. The rest of us simply jump out of our skins. The most hard-boiled and unromantic atheist will surely admit, under torture, to feeling slightly spooked by the eruption of thunder overhead. Scientific types will have none of it. They know thunder to be nothing but 'a big noise following a flash of lightning due to discharge of electricity through the atmosphere'. A description, as scientific ones so often are, which explains everything and that's all. Like 'explaining' music in terms of amplitudes, frequencies and decibels. Emily Dickinson had a scientist friend who solemnly talked her through a sunset as the effect created by viewing a ball of flaming gas from a rotating earth. She replied that when she looked at the sunset she saw 'opal cattle grazing in a sapphire farm'. 'Reversed thunder' is an Emily Dickinson, not a scientific, mode of talk.

Why thunder? What function does it have in the vocabulary of our everyday emotions? Thunder is a hieroglyph of what? It is a goose-bump raising moment that leaves us feeling rather small and exposed, brutally put in our place, fragile and threatened. It is a tap on the shoulder, the cosmic butler's polite cough calling our attention to the fact that our grip on life is not as invincible as we like to think. It is a moment for recalling Job's celebration of thunder as symbol and vehicle for God's voice:

> His thunder announces the coming storm . . .
> At this my heart pounds
> and leaps from its place.

Listen! Listen to the roar of his voice,
to the rumbling that comes from his mouth.
He unleashes his lightning beneath the whole heaven
and sends it to the ends of the earth.
After that comes the sound of his roar;
he thunders with his majestic voice.
When his voice resounds,
he holds nothing back.
God's voice thunders in marvellous ways . . .

(Job 36.33—37.5)

Isn't it rather bizarre, therefore, to suggest any analogy between thunder and prayer? Rather, the two seem to be polar opposites, thunder being everything prayer isn't. A monstrous reverberating din that no one can ignore, contrasting with the soft murmur of voices at prayer behind closed doors that everyone can ignore. But Herbert is not comparing decibel levels, only their potency and authority.

There is a prayer which storms into heaven as unstoppably as thunder storms into our presence on earth. It is the irresistible power of the prayer of love. Prayer inspired by love: love-at-prayer. Prayer not measured by volume or appearances, but by the efficacy of love. Thus, no amount of thundering and storming could cause the cosmos to jump on its hinges the way Jesus' prayer at Calvary did. It was such a small and quiet prayer amongst the rabble noise around the cross, in circumstances of utter desolation. His body convulsing with the agony of slow crucifixion, his mind and spirit obliterated with making atonement for the guilt of the world, he prayed his 'Father, forgive them, for they do not know what they are doing' (Luke 23.34). The answer came as a cataclysmic outpouring of grace-power comparable, if at all, only with the 'Let there be light' of creation itself. The Father answered the Son's prayer, a one-sentence request, and forgave us our God-crucifying iniquity! Such prayer is 'reversed thunder'; heaven is delighted to be defence-less against it, the love of God powerless to resist the prayer of love.

Therefore, if we are searching for practical guidelines into the 'reversed thunder' of the prayer of love, we can turn to Paul's first letter to the Corinthians, chapter 13. For love, read prayer. Thus the opening statement sets down the essential character of love-at-prayer: 'If I speak [pray] in the tongues of men and of angels, but have not love, I am only a resounding gong or a clanging cymbal.' Acts of love are such only as far as we are truly and wholly 'in' or 'behind' them. Thus questions of styles, traditions, and forms of prayer are entirely secondary. Extemporary or book, free-falling unstructured charismatic or 1662 Collect, is an irrelevant debate unless we are ourselves poured into the prayer. As with love, so with love-at-prayer. It requires acts of vigorous sympathetic imagination, an effort to be 'with' and 'in' the people and events named in prayer. Why else should the Lord believe we are sincere?

Jesus called that quality being 'rich towards God' and it is the only wealth Christians should strive for. He contrasted God-ward riches with the more conventional sort amassed by a most conventional person, an insatiably acquisitive 'rich fool' (Luke 12.21). We are thereby forbidden self-absorbed, self-enriching prayer for, say, enhanced sex appeal, large lottery wins, or a flawless physique as an end in itself. The prayers of a person 'rich towards God' move to another rhythm, attuned to love (where love is simply willing the good for others) described as '. . . not self-seeking . . . It always protects, always trusts, always hopes, always perseveres. Love never fails' (1 Corinthians 13.5–8). What will your prayers sound like if cleansed through the filters of practical love? Notice how practical and down to earth love-at-prayer is. Jesus' prayer from the cross was for the most practical need of his executioners – the life-destroying burden of their benighted guilt. Love-at-prayer is potent with God, it is like an 'engine against the Almighty . . . reversed thunder'.

Of course we will pray for ourselves also. The New Testament is clear about the range and motivation for 'me'-prayer. From our heavenly Father we request everything that comes under the concerns of 'our daily bread'. It includes the wherewithal to lead the life God has set each of us to lead: that, and the concomitant gift of freedom from anxiety. Allow no accumulation of anxieties (they are incestuous and fertile breeders) but without delay bring them to the Lord, leave them with him and in exchange 'the peace of God, which transcends all understanding, will guard your hearts and your minds in Christ Jesus' (Philippians 4.7). It was the conviction of that extraordinary man Hudson Taylor, the pioneer missionary leader in China, that missionaries could keep their sanity under killing pressures only on the strength of that principle. 'The Lord's will is that all his people should be an unburdened people, fully supplied, strong, healthy and happy.' If that smacks of a too easy triumphalism, read how he and his fellowship of workers went through hell and high water in nineteenth-century China by it.

Jesus said, 'Do not worry about your life' (Matthew 6.25–34). His word for 'worry' suggests legitimate concerns allowed to run to over-kill. Be 'rich toward God' by being free enough to serve and pray for others in love. Free from self-obsession, from the spirit of this 'hedonistic ice-age' in which we live. The promised blessing is an authentic lightness of heart.

And prayer is the '***Christ-side-piercing spear.***'

Christians of whatever tradition will agree that vital and authentic prayer is that which reaches into the heart of Christ, or however one wishes to express it. The first person to do that was not a saint, a mystic, or an apostle but a Roman soldier in the execution squad. Whether out of casual brutality or as an act of mercy he 'pierced Jesus' side with a spear, and at once there was a flow of blood and water' (John 19.34). Avoiding the subtleties of Eucharistic symbol- ism we can say plainly that the outflow of blood and water was the outflow of Jesus' life. With enormous imaginative power, George Herbert sees our prayer as that spear piercing Christ's side, pene- trating deep into his innermost body, his heart, releasing the flow of his inexhaustible life into the world.

It is fascinating to speculate how such a highly charged, awesome picture came into his mind. Herbert would have been aware of the cult of 'Christ's wounds' that flourished in England and on the continent right up to the Reformation. In spite of the efforts of reforming iconoclasts, many parish churches retained and displayed the iconography of the wounds, the implements of Christ's passion, his scourging, crucifixion and the spear thrust, to aid worshippers in their meditations. In his poem 'Good Friday' Herbert speaks about 'Thy whips, thy nails, thy wounds, thy woes'. In the cult of the Five Wounds, and of the Holy Name, the devotee contemplated the passion of Jesus in minute and ghastly detail. The basic statement that 'Jesus died for our sins' deserves to be felt deeply, slowly, and often. Through emphasis on the real sufferings of their Lord, men and women gained confidence to see in him a close brother. This form of adoration celebrated the sweetness, tenderness and accessibility of the truly human divine redeemer. The believer was emboldened to claim kinship with Jesus, whose wounds were an hieroglyph for his loving intimate solidarity with people whose own lives were often a harsh and brutal affair. Such contemplation became the dynamic for compassion towards others. In a poem of the time the suffering Jesus tells his people to 'See me, be kind'. A popular prayer ran:

> O good Jesus, how sweet you are in the heart of one who thinks upon you and loves you . . . sweeter in that which is humble than in that which is exalted . . . it is sweeter to view you as dying before the Jews on the tree, than as holding sway over the angels in heaven; *to see you as a man bearing every aspect of human nature to the end*, than as God manifesting divine nature, to see you as the dying redeemer than as the invisible creator.[1]

In Devotion to the Wounds, the worshipper contemplated each wound in turn and what it will have cost Jesus to endure it, then turning reflection into prayer that the grace and power of the wounds might inflame the hearts of faithful people to love of God. The spear-wound in the side held particular fascination for the devotee because it opened a way into the Lord's heart. They found in the side-wound a symbol of refuge within Christ's saving, protecting love. Julian of Norwich saw there 'a fair and delectable place and large enough for all mankind that shall be saved, and rest in peace and love'.

Such was the devotional atmosphere leading into Herbert's time. He took up that rich seam of imaginative contemplation, giving it a startling extension: what the spear-thrust did to Jesus on the cross, our prayers do now. They are a 'Christ-side-piercing spear'. In prayer we enter the heart of Jesus, an action that releases the outpouring of his life for the world. It is an astounding metaphor. What can it mean for the way we pray?

First, it heals a deep spiritual anxiety, one which casts its shadow over our joy in prayer. It is the crisis we feel in being people of flesh trying to communicate with the God who 'lives in unapproachable light' (1 Timothy 6.16). On a good day and in the right mood it is possible to feel that, yes, our prayers are getting through to God; but that is a fragile balance and we are soon undone by the sheer discrepancy between God's searing holiness and our own flesh-ness. Theologians lecture us to approach the Almighty Father with reverential awe for his transcendent 'otherness' but, frankly, that language merely serves to exacerbate the problem.

The gospel is that God has in Christ approached us from out of his 'unapproachable light'. He has crossed the divine–human divide to identify himself with our flesh in the miracle of Christ's incarna-tion '... to make our joy complete' (1 John 1.1–4). An Ascension Day hymn of the ancient church puts it with blunt power:

> The flesh offends, the flesh atones;
> the flesh of God now reigns as God.

We touch God in prayer not on the side of his 'unapproachable light' but in his flesh, our flesh, which he has made his flesh in Christ. We touch God in 'the flesh of God' as our prayers enter like a spear-thrust through Christ's open side into his heart. He offers himself to our prayers as he offered his side to their spear-thrust. How blessedly different this is to those lofty abstractions of the theologians which effectively leave God out of our flesh-experience.

Now use this picture to assure your anxious mind that God stands open, touchable, and accessible to our prayers in Christ. 'The flesh of God' is our touching-place. He said, 'Touch me and see; a ghost does not have flesh and bones, as you see I have' (Luke 24.39).

Second, consider the Christ-life (blood and water), which flows out in response to the spear-thrust of our prayers. It flows from the heart of him 'who has been tempted in every way, just as we are – yet was without sin' (Hebrews 4.15). In Jesus God became an 'insider', standing with us on the 'inside' of human experience. The God of 'unapproachable light' would always remain the outsider in relation to our flesh-ness. Therefore in order to know us and to understand our experience he set aside his power and limited himself to such a degree that he was genuinely able to feel our life on the inside. Jesus' three temptations in the desert at the beginning of his public ministry occurred *after* he had allowed himself to sink into the weakness, physical and psychological, of prolonged malnutrition (Matthew 4.2). How very strange, that he should prepare for his duel with Satan by weakening himself!

To qualify as our practical saviour, Christ had to feel, taste, know experimentally what it is like as a human being trying to do the will of God in this world. Urs von Balthasar remarks that 'God does the unthinkable: *he exposes himself to Satan's fascination, in order to burst the dazzling bubble from within.'* Therefore the heart we touch, and the life which flows to us from it, is 'omnipotent sympathy'. Sympathy, in the deepest sense of one who suffers with us, as an insider with us, but also *omnipotent* sympathy, an omnipotent fellow-feeling with us gained by living as a genuine human being. Otherwise he would be like those well-meaning but essentially fraudulent people who play at identification with the poor when at any time they can slip home for a bath, a good meal, and a night between fresh sheets. They cannot know the anxiety, the sheer grinding worry of not having enough, therefore they cannot sympathize in the full biblical sense of that over-used word. But Christ, our insider, felt full temptation to doubt, to worry, to throw in the towel – but he overcame. Our prayers touch his heart and draw out his 'I know. Trust me. I will bring you through.'

A third aspect of prayer as the 'Christ-side-piercing spear', following from the previous two points, is that Jesus is our brother in the profound Hebrew sense of the term. 'Both the one who makes men holy and those who are made holy are of the same family. So Jesus is not ashamed to call them brothers' (Hebrews 2.11). In the culture of the Old Testament people depended upon the strengths and the loyalties of kinship for survival. In that network of relatives you hoped for a *Go'el*, 'kinsman-redeemer', your nearest able-bodied relative whose responsibility it was to bail you out in times of hardship. If you had lost your cow, your field, or fallen into debt, or had suffered at the hands of an enemy, your Go'el relative was duty-bound to come to your rescue. He would take on your difficulties and make them his own personal concern: pay your debts, get you out of slavery if need be, restore your possessions, fight your battles, defeat your enemies, even avenge your death. When it is said, 'Jesus is not ashamed to call them brothers', it means he accepts all the responsibilities of being our Go'el.

When we call to him, in prayer, thrusting deep into his heart, the 'blood and water', which flow to us, are all the strength of our Go'el-brother. The point is this: it is in the Go'el's job description that he must, and therefore we can depend upon it that he will, undertake to set us upright, restored to life, set on our way. By prayer we draw upon all the insider fellow feeling, and the over-coming power of Christ our Go'el, in his unbreakable solidarity with us.

CHAPTER 8

The six-days world transposing in an hour

At the risk of overloading the imagination and blowing all the fuses, try to visualize this: a world which took God 'six days' to create is changed, transformed, 'transposing' (as in a shift of key in music) in the space of 'an hour'. It was Christ's 'hour' of his passion and resurrection that released indescribable energies to lift the world's guilt and heal the rift between God and his children. 'An hour' in which Jesus broke the satanic 'principalities and powers' oppressing the human family. 'An hour', therefore, which makes 'transposing' possible, energizing the transposition of the world from a condition of 'Paradise Lost' to the potential for Paradise Regained.

Prayer speaks the language of the 'hour' and of the 'transposing'. It flows out of the one and celebrates the other. In prayer we invoke the authority of Christ's 'hour' and follow the logic of his 'transposing' work in the world. Everything we ask for in prayer, everyone we pray for, it is to bring all into the renewal of Christ's transposing of the world. In fact prayer, says George Herbert, is 'the six-days world transposing in an hour'. In its subtle way, is this the most profound picture so far of the dynamic and the purpose of prayer?

Pupils of a London Rabbi asked him one day what he made of the Christians' claim that Messiah came two thousand years ago. He went to the classroom window, opened it, stared intently up and down the street for several minutes, and then replied, 'It doesn't look like it.' Overawed by Herbert's stunning view of prayer, what it achieves and what it is based upon, we may feel we side with the Rabbi on this one. Frankly the world we experience most days of the week doesn't look very 'transposed'. We have been here before in chapter five, and the same question relating to the 'hiddenness' of the kingdom of God. In this present age Christ's victory – his kingdom and his 'transposing' – are 'veiled manifestations' accessible only to the eye of faith, utterly real but concealed. Any uncertainty on our part over the reality of Christ's 'transposing' work subverts prayer. We must try to settle this question for our peace of mind and joy in prayer.

The question is – to put it as plainly as we can – if Christ broke the satanic power by his 'hour' of the cross and resurrection, how can we account for present wickedness and the demonic in the world? Indeed the forces of evil seem if anything to grow more audacious and ingenious with the passing of time. If this is a pressing question for us, how much more was it for those young churches in Asia Minor towards the end of the first century AD, conscious of the Domitian persecution boiling up over their heads. Where is Christ's victory over Satan while Caesar (Hitler, Stalin, Pol Pot, Milosevic, etc.) is slaughtering the innocent?

We find the answer in Revelation chapter 12. It opens with what is the essence of spiritual warfare on earth, with all the appearance of a hopelessly unequal contest: a pregnant woman against a dragon (12.1–4). Nothing could be more defenceless than this mother and her newborn child. She is the messianic community, the Church, and her labour pains are the dangers and sufferings endured by the true Israel as they await the advent of their kingly redeemer (Galatians 4.24–7). She is the Church in touch with 'the powers of the coming age' (Hebrews 6.5).

Facing the woman, and ready to pounce on the Christ-child, is the dragon, the serpent, the devil, Satan (Revelation 12.9). He is God's ancient enemy, the disrupter of creation, the great deceiver, all voracious greed, heads, horns, claws and teeth. The dragon is in fact described in terms characteristic of its earthly agents, which are politico-military powers. Thus also Daniel's creatures symbolize the four great empires of his world (Daniel 7.1–8), and Jeremiah similarly sketched Nebuchadnezzar as a serpent, which swallowed Jerusalem whole and spat out the debris (Jeremiah 51.34). Adam earlier had dealings with their notorious progenitor.

The Satan-dragon must, above all things, snuff out the threat to his domination posed by the woman's Christ-child. As God continuously creates the cosmos, Satan strives to destroy it. As God created all things good and beautiful, the devil distorts and perverts them. God plants a field of wheat, and the devil strews it with weeds. Above all else, Satan strives to dishonour and discredit God, to deface his image in humankind.

Imagine, then, the demonic fury when there appears in the midst of the human family an individual who perfectly carries the divine image in his truly human nature. He does so on behalf of all humanity and as their saving representative. Hence the chaotic panic in the fallen spiritual world of 'rulers and powers' (Ephesians 6.12). Small wonder the dragon 'stood in front of the woman who was about to give birth, so that he might devour her child the moment it was born' (Revelation 12.4).

Satan storms at the messianic community, the Church, and her child. The awesome flare-up of demonic activity provoked by Christ's presence in his ministry witnesses to the reality of God's invasion of satanic territory (e.g., Mark 1.21—2.12). This child has come to 'rule all the nations with an iron sceptre' (Revelation 12.5) and the satanic empire is reeling.

The contest between the Satan-dragon and the child appears hopelessly one-sided. 'Our struggle is not against flesh and blood, but against the rulers, against the authorities, against the powers of this dark world and against the spiritual forces of evil in the heavenly realms' (Ephesians 6.12). The manifold 'rulers and powers' (and the whole galaxy of fallen demonic beings) unfold out of the one Satan-power. They exercise their being by taking possession of the world as a whole, and of individual men and women, the elements, political and social institutions, and religious trends. Above all, their possession is exercised mainly through the 'atmosphere', which is the immediate site of their power. Ephesians 2.2 speaks of 'the ruler of the kingdom of the air, the spirit who is now at work in those who are disobedient', graphically suggesting soft atheism as something in the air we breathe.

There is a power, which overcomes the Great Disrupter, but is so extraordinary that Satan himself utterly misunderstood it. To the hate-ridden demonic mind, Christ had surely fallen totally under his enemies' control when they nailed him to the cross. Now surely, the dragon devours the child-redeemer. Crucifixion not only killed its victim but also utterly humiliated him, obliterating his reputation. Crucifixion allowed the caprice and sadism of the executioners full rein. On the cross the total force of satanic spite slammed into Christ's defenceless body. 'The enemies of Christianity always referred to the disgracefulness of the death of Jesus with great emphasis and malicious pleasure' (Hengel).[1]

But the cross totally outwitted Satan. It has a wisdom and a power incomprehensible to the fallen spiritual powers (1 Corinthians 2.8). Thus an event, which happened in AD 33 outside Jerusalem, is described by John in terms of its impact in the spiritual realm: 'And there was war in heaven' (Revelation 12.7). The chaos-dragon, in its serial incarnations from Babylon to Rome and down to our own times, is defeated and ruined by the Christ it crucified (vv. 7–9). It is a moment, or 'an hour', precisely marked with the hymn beginning '*Now* have come the salvation and the power and the kingdom of our God' (v. 10). Christians believe that world history hinges on what happened in Christ's 'hour'.

And yet evil thrives. Was it a real victory, or was it, as the critics of Christianity like to suggest, the Church's fantasy? A fundamental and decisive change in the structure of creation did occur in 'an hour', but God has allowed the defeated Satan to exist, pictured in Revelation 12 as a damaged creature 'hurled down' (v. 9). The effect of the cross on Satan is to provoke him to behave like a fatally wounded reptile which, in its rage, frenzy and panic becomes even more terrifying in its death throes, lashing out in all directions, 'filled with fury, because he knows that his time is short' (v. 12).

'Time' is Satan's dilemma; time running out, his life running out. Ejected from the eternity of God's presence (v. 8) he is unable to exist in any place (or person) where Christ dwells; he is ever driven out from those places where people live under the sign of Christ (v. 11 and 7.2, 3). Satan is trapped in time and in his fear he rages against time passing away (12.12). To switch metaphors, if the manager of a store knows that his crooked practices are about to be exposed, his anxiety will affect the atmosphere around him. Time is ticking away; he stands to lose everything, and the people around him can feel it. The spirit of the present age is something like that.

Paradoxically, the increasing ferocity of demonic activity in our time is the sign of a defeated Satan!

To summarize: Christ decisively defeated Satan in his 'hour'. Where men and women believe in Jesus they share in the cry of joy that permeates the New Testament: 'Christ has died, Christ is risen, the power of Satan has been broken!' But God allows the Evil One to continue in existence fatally wounded, crazed with frustration, its time running out. Take him with utmost seriousness because his remaining destructiveness is directed against the Church. Satan loathes and fears the Church for her truth. She is entrusted with the truth that sets the world free. Only the Church understands what is going on in the cosmic warfare, she can name names, she can expose Satan for the doomed and damned creature he is, she holds divine revelation, the scriptures, under the Holy Spirit of 'wisdom and revelation'. She worships and proclaims 'our Saviour, Christ Jesus, who has destroyed death and has brought life and immortality to light through the gospel' (2 Timothy 1.10). Satan dreads the Church when she is true to her truth, '. . . the light of the world. A city on a hill cannot be hidden' (Matthew 5.14).

Notice carefully the significance for us of the next image in the Revelation 12 vision. The mortally damaged serpent pursues 'the woman' spewing a jet of water out of its mouth to 'sweep her away with the torrent' (vv. 13–15). It spews a torrent of lies, negative propaganda, malicious rumours (think of the glee with which the national media seize upon instances of Christian failure or decline in church attendance figures) to discredit Christ and his truth incarnated in Christian people. It is a war of ideas for hearts and minds and the Church is in the middle of it: the focus of it. This is the point: a Church which holds the truth entrusted to her, constantly meditating in it and applying it in practice, teaching and proclaiming it, is essential to the wholeness of a society. 'You are the salt of the earth.' But we can expect the forces of darkness to hate us for it. *Prayer for the world should begin with prayer for the Church to be true to her truth.*

We need protection. Christ has set his Name upon us: 'In my Name they will drive out demons' (Mark 16.17). The salvific, protecting power of the Name is fundamental to effective Christian living within current spiritual warfare. We use it in our prayers and constantly invoke it for blessing. The Name is our defence against the stream of deceits spewed out by the serpent 'to overtake the woman and sweep her away with the torrent'. We routinely (though too often thoughtlessly) claim the authority of the Name at the end of every prayer: '. . . this we ask in Jesus name. Amen.' Upgrade that customary cliché into an invocation of Christ's power to save and keep against the attention of the infuriated rulers and powers. Sometimes we sing the Name:

> I bind unto myself today
> The strong name of the Trinity,
> By invocation of the same,
> The three in One and One in three . . .
> I bind unto myself today
> The power of God to hold and keep,
> His eye to watch, His might to stay,
> His ear to hearken to my need . . .
> Christ be with me, Christ within me,
> Christ behind me, Christ before me,
> Christ beside me, Christ to win me,
> Christ to comfort and restore me,
> Christ beneath me, Christ above me
> Christ in quiet, Christ in danger . . .
> I bind unto myself the name,
> The strong name of the Trinity,
> By invocation of the same . . .
>
> ('St Patrick's Breastplate')[2]

We are saying that in the struggle to hold to, and to communicate the truth of, Christ, prayer is first a deliberate clothing of the Church with the protecting name of Christ. Against the vast and insidious outpouring of illusions and distortions in the life of our society only such prayer will guard the mind and hold us faithful, strong, clear and resourceful in the Truth.

It follows that our prayers for Christ's transposing of the world will have a dimension of 'deliverance' about them. When we pray for one another we will surely remember to invoke the power of the Name over our minds against the entrance (a subtle osmosis) of semi-truth and compromise. A friend from Singapore tells me of congregations there, full of bright young business people, who routinely spend the first hour or so of their worship time in open prayer directed against demonic activity which besets individuals and society. It conjures a wonderful picture of the power of the Name invoked within a world leader in IT excellence. Usually it is over-simplistic to transfer the experiences and practices of churches in one part of the world directly into churches in vastly different cultures in other parts. But we can safely emulate their awareness of spiritual warfare and their primitive application of prayer in Christ's powerful name.

We are talking of the place of prayer within Christ's work of 'transposing' the world into the liberty of the children of God. Prayer for that movement, we have said, is bound up with prayer for the 'truthfulness' of the Church. And that in turn involves us in spiritual warfare. In this situation we are commanded, 'Be controlled and alert' (1 Peter 5.8), where 'controlled' means 'freed from illusions' (the old version has, 'Be sober and watch'). Controlled, or sober-minded, implies that we be fully aware of the rulers and powers, their ferocious hatred of the Church as 'a light in a dark world', without being intimidated by the menace of the demonic. Alongside that injunction is a second crucial word: 'test [discern] the spirits' (1 John 4.1).

Before we spend our energies attempting to witness to Christ's truth against the darkness of the world, first hold back and by prayer 'discern the spirits'. Awaken, guard, and practise the charisma of discernment of the spirits. It is a gift of the Holy Spirit for the wisdom of the Church (1 Corinthians 14.1). It is the spiritual ability to look into the world and tell good from bad, malign spiritual activity from the harmless or helpful. Where we lack the gift we are in danger of misreading the situation, like the folk who see demons in every cupboard and around every corner, responsible for all spilt milk and every blown fuse. We may, then, fail to recognize the demonic when it really occurs. We must pray continually for one another to 'discern the spirits'.

May I mention in conclusion two personal examples to illustrate the need to exercise the charisma of 'discerning the spirits' in prayer. The first was a personal experience; the second is a degree of discernment I have recently encountered, to which I am still very much an outsider, hoping to get on the inside.

More exactly the personal experience illustrates the dangers of a stubborn *non-discernment* of the spirits! It derives from an evening spent in a Malay village witnessing a 'Main-Petri' ceremony of exorcism. As the Bomor Hantu, the spirit-wizard, crooned his incantations to the 'malign spirit' in that troubled woman, I realized that I felt more at home among those folk than I do among the well-heeled atheists of my own society! As a Christian I have more in common with that dreamy people who take seriously the fact that their lives are open to the higher powers of the invisible spirit world, than with many of my fellow citizens who are embarrassed by any reference to their personal spiritual lives.

Those Islamic-animists believed in the reality of spiritual powers impinging on human beings; so do I. They turned to a mediator, their spirit-doctor, to deal with the invisible on their behalf; so do I, his name is Jesus. They believe sacrifices and offerings are necessary in order to approach the higher powers; so do I, 'the blood of Christ cleanses us from all sin'. I understand their worldview; I see where they are coming from. But of our own Western European/North American-type culture, the late Cardinal Thomas Winning of Glasgow declared in his forceful way that it breeds 'spiritual dwarfs'. What common ground do I have with the western secularist mind with its low spiritual ceiling, its dull, boring materialistic worldview (we shouldn't mistake sentimentality – we have oceans of it sloshing around in our culture! – with authentic God-seeking spirituality) in thrall to the felt here-and-now?

But that observation brings me to the point of the exorcism story: I am in danger of projecting what I like about *it* on to what I find *here* in my own society. 'Spiritual warfare' was virtually synonymous for me with certain phenomena of spirit possession. I like witches' covens, centres of voodooism, all the paraphernalia of occultism, and the rest of it; *but is that 'discerning the spirits'?* When I prayerfully, and hopefully under the guidance of the Spirit, look into our own culture as it is, I see not the phenomena of eastern spiritism, but an earth-dream, an illusion. Satan, 'the father of lies', is the master illusionist, able to distort reality in our minds. We have illusion taking two extreme and apparently opposite forms: the illusion of unbridled hedonism – the meaning of life is more and more choice of more and more pleasurable experiences – and the illusion of desolation – life is bleak and sad.

In the 'mission field' of our own society we encounter on every hand, and in spite of unprecedented affluence, a sense of gloom, nameless fears and anxiety, the terrible sense of insecurity of soul; meaninglessness created by the sheer scale and dynamism of financial forces, the various oppressions that batten down on people's minds. These are the new as well as the old demons enslaving men and women today, including folk who sit in the pews of our churches. First, 'discern the spirits' as they actually are, not as I might wish them to be. Next we ask how do those spirits, which appear as illusions of pleasure and of despair, resist Christ's 'transposing' of the world? The direction of our prayers then becomes clear.

Thus we will pray that the entire activity of Christian teaching, worship, prayer, faith, caring, and so on, will contain enough realism (realism to oppose illusion) to take a grip on troubled minds.

The second example of 'prayerful discernment' is something I came upon quite recently in one of Charles Williams' novels. He covenanted with a group of friends to take seriously the injunction, 'Carry each other's burdens, and in this way you will fulfil the law of Christ' (Galatians 6.2). They believed it means more than just praying for each other, however conscientiously, in the usual sense. Quite simply, if you carry my burden, then I am left with no burden to carry – that is 'the law of Christ'. The group shared with each other the details of their respective burdens, how they experienced the burden, with what sensations of fear, anxiety, dread, stress, the sense of the burden came upon them, at what time of the day and where. That is, they first practised 'discerning the spirits' which were oppressing one another, and then used those insights to practise what Williams called 'the doctrine of substituted love'. Thus I might covenant with you to imaginatively enter into your burden at 11.30 a.m. tomorrow morning when it tends to oppress you particularly strongly. I will visualize your situation as you have described it to me, and I will open up to feel the load of the 'burden'. But you for your part must, at 11.30 a.m. tomorrow morning, relinquish your hold on that burden. If I am carrying it, you no longer have a burden to carry.

In his novel *Descent into Hell*, Williams describes a young woman, Pauline, who all her life has been stalked . . . by herself! She hears footsteps behind, glances back and there she is, her exact self. The experience is driving her steadily mad. Stanhope, the man she confides in, is amazed that she hasn't practised 'substituted love' with a friend and covenants to 'carry her burden' for her. She describes precisely the process of the thing so that he can 'discern the spirit' and enter into her distress in his imagination. He tells her what to expect – 'When you hear the footsteps behind you look back. "She" will be there as usual, but you will know that I am carrying your fear, and if I have your fear, you are left with no fear.' 'Discerning the spirits' in that sense means we act as Christ for each other.

Incidentally, with the fear lifted, and the awareness of her strong friend consciously at that moment carrying it instead of her, Pauline is unafraid to confront the other 'self-spirit' stalking her. It turns out to be her true self – a self full of joy. 'It had been her incapacity for joy, nothing else, that had till now turned the vision of herself aside.'[3]

CHAPTER 9

A kind of tune, which all things hear and fear

Our teacher has music on his mind. In the previous metaphor prayer is the world 'transposing' into a different key; now it is 'a kind of tune'; universally heard and 'feared', as respect, or as dread. His biographer mentions that Herbert's 'chiefest recreation was music, in which heavenly art he was a most excellent master, and did himself compose many divine hymns and anthems which he set and sung to his lute or viol'. Twice a week he walked into Salisbury to attend worship at the cathedral, occasions he referred to as 'his heaven on earth'.

I imagine him walking along the lanes and across the meadows from Bemerton to Salisbury, hearing 'a kind of tune' coming out from the cathedral – bells, orchestras, organ, choirs, chanting and singing. Did the experience suggest to his mind prayer as something already on the move in the air around him, inviting his prayer? You may recall an earlier reference to this in the metaphor of prayer as 'Angels' age' (p. 8). When we pray our words enter a cosmos already pulsating with angelic adoration, the universe set shuddering on its hinges by their ecstasy.

There is no question where the cosmic hymn originates: at the empty tomb. As though the angel struck a tuning fork and stood it on 'the great stone' rolled back, sending its note singing through all space and time: Christ is risen! Prayer as 'a kind of tune which all things hear and fear' is first and last Christ's prayer. He stands in the midst of his earthly family gathering us up into his worship offered eternally to the Father:

Christ Jesus, High Priest of the New and Eternal Covenant, taking human nature, introduced into this earthly exile that hymn which is sung throughout all ages in the halls of heaven. He joins the entire community of mankind to himself, associating it with his own singing of this canticle of divine praise.

For he continues his priestly work through the agency of his church, which is ceaselessly engaged in praising the Lord and interceding for the salvation of the whole world.[1]

All prayer derives from Christ's canticle of the resurrection. That excellent description also suggests how 'all things hear' the prayer, Christ's and ours: Christians carry it with them wherever they go in their working lives, unconsciously, like incense in the texture of their clothes and in their hair. Our Sundays at worship among the congregation are times when our lives are drenched, once more, with Christ's canticle of praise to the Father.

George Herbert took that idea of life scented with prayer even further. He had discovered it was the only defence against the creeping paralysis of spiritual sterility, when the heart hardens into dry, barren formality and hypocrisy. To be real the canticle must first be felt and lived, heart-deep, wholly given to God. Merely being among the congregation is not enough. Only Christ himself can draw us to himself and into his prayer. Only he can keep the believer in a condition of continuous renewal and vitality. Herbert learned to plunge his mind into the fulness of two words: '*My Master*'.

> How sweetly doth *My Master* sound! *My Master*!
>   As Ambergris leaves a rich scent
>   Unto the taster:
>   So do these words a sweet content,
> An oriental fragrancy, *My Master*.
>
> With these all day I do perfume my mind,
>   My mind ev'n thrust into them both . . .
>   ('The Odour')

To the Christ-enchanted mind the world only makes sense if it, too, is caught up into Christ's ceaseless praise to the Father. Thus Herbert's call:

> Let all the world in ev'ry corner sing,
> > *My God and King.*
> > > ('Antiphon' 1)

The world is gifted to comply with that plea. The incarnation and resurrection of the Son of God altered everything. From it we receive a new destiny, but so also has creation. The physical universe, of which we are part, is being taken up into the very life of God himself, transfigured into indescribable splendour. The last vision in scripture is of 'a new heaven *and* a new earth' (Revelation 21.1). In our rush towards the new heaven we overlook the wonder of a new earth, which is as much part of our future. The transformation of the human family and the glorification of the material creation are already under way.

Creation is not silent on its way towards becoming 'a new earth'. The psalmist is convinced 'the heavens declare the glory of God; the skies proclaim the work of his hands. Day after day they pour forth speech' (Psalm 19.1–2). And 'all you have made will praise you, O Lord' (Psalm 145.10). It would be very odd if so much could be going on in creation without us ever feeling its touch and tremor. But of course we do; those who stand open before the world, attentive and teachable, will detect 'a kind of tune'. On occasions it can be almost unbearably moving. A young woman working in the entertainment industry, dispirited by the tawdriness around her, took a break and went for a stroll:

> It was a glorious sunny evening and I walked through the park and sat down by the water intending to read. I never opened my book. It was very beautiful with the sun glinting through the trees and the ducks swimming on the water, and quite suddenly I felt lifted beyond all the turmoil and the conflict. There was no visual image and I knew I was sitting on a seat in the park but I felt as if I was lifted above the world and looking down on it. The disillusion and cynicism were gone and I felt compassion

suffusing my whole being, compassion for all the people of earth. I was possessed by a peace that I have never felt before or since, and – what is to me most interesting and curious of all – this whole state was not emotional: it was as if I was not without emotion but beyond it . . . The experience passed off gradually, and I suppose it lasted about 20 to 30 minutes. At the time I felt it was an experience of God, because I interpreted it according to my own religious framework.[2]

Thus in singing to its Lord the world also witnesses to men and women. We feel the world turned towards us, reaching out, calling to us, it has wisdom to share with us if we will attend. Always, it seems, creation is pointing to another place beyond itself. Another typical experience is recorded by a young man climbing in Scotland:

> I was climbing first and was ahead of my companions. The roar of a waterfall nearby was deafening, until I climbed over the rim of the rock face. In absolute quiet, within a beautiful scenic panorama, I found God. The description of Samadhi fits my experience perfectly. I was no longer aware of 'myself'; and yet I retained my personality. This was however merged into an infinite corporate personality of all life. Peace, love and understanding became real and tangible.[3]

Those are moments when nature's communion with God (and we are part of her) is palpable. Then she seems to smile, inviting us to share in and make use of her prayer. A beautiful expression of the experience is in Patrick Kavanagh's poem, 'Canal Bank Walk':

> Leafy-with-love banks and the green waters of the canal
> Pouring redemption for me, that I do
> The will of God, wallow in the habitual, the banal,
> Grow with nature again as before I grew.
> The bright stick trapped, the breeze adding a third
> Party to the couple kissing on an old seat,
> And a bird gathering materials for the nest for the Word

Eloquently new and abandoned to its delirious beat.
O unworn world enrapture me, encapture me in a web
Of fabulous grass and eternal voices by a beech,
Feed the gaping need of my senses, give me ad lib
To pray unselfconsciously with overflowing speech
For this soul needs to be honoured with a new dress woven
From green and blue things and arguments that cannot be
   proven.[4]

These are creation's sudden and surprising gifts in a world turned praising towards her Lord, uttering her 'kind of tune which all things hear and fear'. But a steady bombardment of irreverence and derision threatens to overwhelm her canticle, or rather, our ability to detect it. She looks to us for our partnership, indeed for our leadership, in the work of praise.

Thus from the outset Adam came to creation's assistance by 'naming' the animals. God had appointed him priest-mediator in the world; his first task was to release creation from its incoherent jumble by telling each its 'name' and thereby its place and purpose in the order of things. Herbert neatly pictures our mediatorial function:

> Of all the creatures both in sea and land
> Only to man thou hast made known thy ways
> And put the pen alone into his hand,
> And made him secretary of thy praise.

> ('Providence')

In Psalm 148, Israel as choir leader calls upon all creation, from the galaxies to snowflakes, to join in the hymn of praise. We are therefore, as God's priestly people in the world, implicated in creation's ability to sing her song. Only we have language, 'the pen alone in our hand' as secretary of God's praise. What does this mean in practice?

We will honour the world as a sacred theophany, teeming with God's self-revelations. 'The whole earth is full of his glory' (Isaiah 6.3). It is in our priestly responsibility in creation to protect its integrity as a God-praising order. To argue for the symbolic and sacramental nature of the world as a place luminous with the love and power of God. To alert all who will listen to creation's canticle. To practise in our own lives what we urge upon others – put our ear to the heart of things, open our dull eyes and notice what is there. Elizabeth Barratt Browning had a pithy rebuke for our somnambulism: 'The earth is ablaze with the fire of God, but only those who see it take their shoes off; the rest sit around and pick blackberries.' The world's canticle, its way of singing 'My God and King', mingles with our prayer and together they are drawn up into Christ's High Priestly worship to the Father.

We will conclude this meditation by noticing one particular aspect of creation's 'kind of tune' – beauty, and the way ugliness threatens to smother beauty's witness to the beautiful God. George Herbert was clear about the origin and mission of beauty in the world. He encountered it supremely in language:

> . . . sweet phrases, lovely metaphors . . .
> Lovely enchanting language, sugar cane,
> Honey of roses . . .
> True beauty dwells on high: ours is a flame
> But borrowed thence to light us thither.
> Beauty and beauteous words should go together.
>
> ('The Forerunners')

The beautiful God should be celebrated beautifully. It was a war-cry in the early church that 'Everything good, everything beautiful belongs to us' (Justin). Beautiful things whisper their 'kind of tune', their witness to the loveliness of their Lord. It is part of our stewardship to promote and celebrate the beautiful as pointers to God; and to be on our guard against the cult of ugliness and pessimism out of which no canticle rises to God. A critic at the 49th Venice Biennale reported on the impression of gloom and wilful ugliness in much of the exhibition:

The Italian Pavilion contains several other unfamiliar artists. Ene-Liis Semper, a young newcomer from Estonia, plays a dejected, crop-haired woman in a grainy black-and-white video installation called FF/REW. After reading disconsolately at a table, she gets up, puts a noose around her neck, and kicks over the stool supporting her feet. Respite is offered as the footage goes into reverse, taking her back to the table. But she then attempts another suicide with a gun, and finally succeeds in hanging herself again . . . Paul Graham's photographs likewise take us into an arena we would prefer to avoid: the graffiti-strewn walls of public lavatories, where desperate loners scrawl details of their sexual longings. Against all the odds, Graham's dark-toned images often take on the eloquence of paintings.[5]

Against mainstream, institutionalized, well-heeled despair (we can detect no prayer to God from their world) we will take our stand on a creation which even at this moment is undergoing the glorification of Christ's resurrection:

> *All things therefore are charged with love, are charged with God and if we know how to touch them give off sparks and take fire, yield drops and flow, ring and tell of him.*

(Hopkins)[6]

CHAPTER 10

Softness, and peace, and joy, and love, and bliss

The loveliest sounds in the whole sonnet are in this line. A cluster of five small facets, simple and enchanted, it reads like a poetic child's description of a moonlit walk through snow. Lovers, also, are known to use expressions similar to 'softness, and peace, and joy, and love, and bliss'.

Had George Herbert spoken of prayer more conventionally as, say, 'true, and right, and good, and wise' we would have no choice but to take his word for it. But 'softness, and peace, and joy, and love, and bliss' are felt qualities, either we know them through the senses or they cannot be known at all. They are taken in through the skin and the body, as well as through the mind. 'Softness . . . and bliss' carry their own conviction and the evidence of their reality with them like a scent, a kiss, a sacrament.

Some readers may wish to bale out at this point. Some believe the idea of prayer as a sensuous experience should carry a severe health warning. Did we not take in with our mother's milk the principle that in matters of faith 'feelings' are not to be trusted an inch? We were taught to take our stand on what God has said in scripture about prayer and not on the state of our moods and emotions when praying. The wisdom of that advice is unassailable, and yet numbers of us have discovered over the years that prayer can become a chilly, cerebral affair, strong on the knowledge of biblical foundations for prayer, but emotionally threadbare. Is it credible that the Holy 'Spirit of wisdom and revelation' would enlighten our inner world, to 'give us the light of the knowledge of the glory of God in the face of Christ' (Ephesians 1.17; 2 Corinthians 4.6) without it registering throughout our psychological and emotional life?

Herbert doesn't think so. There is an experience of God in prayer that can be described as 'softness, and peace, and joy, and love, and bliss'. Perhaps our ways of knowing and encountering the Lord need to expand to respond to the full repertoire and range of his self-revelation.

If certain traditions frown on the emotions, others do something similar with the intellect. But any split between reason and our spiritual–emotional–psychological gifts is damaging. Yet at times one will take the lead and the other follow. If, for example, we were attempting to solve calculus then presumably our powers of reasoning would take the lead. But in this matter of receiving the divine touch in prayer, when something like 'softness . . . and bliss' are part of the psychic vocabulary used between the Spirit and ourselves, clearly other powers and gifts come into play.

The distinction between the rational and intuitive aspects of our make-up goes by various names. Most commonly we talk of the 'masculine' and the 'feminine' principles. Another term is 'anima' (the feminine principle) and 'animus' (the masculine). Animus, our masculine side, is associated with power, the warrior, the savage, the tyrant, the problem-solver, and the controlling tendency. Its aim is to rule the self and acquire knowledge. Its type of love is eros. Anima, the feminine principle in our mode of knowing, we associate with gifts of intuition and perception (which earlier we called knowing 'through the skin and the body'). It is at home in the deep imagination and its love is like agape, self-effacing and self-surrendering.

In relation to prayer the most intriguing and suggestive description I know of the way animus and anima compete within us is in Paul Claudel's parable:

All is not going well in the home of Animus and Anima. It is a long time since their short honeymoon, during which Anima had the right of speaking at her ease, while Animus listened to her ravished with delight. After all, did not the household live on the fortune brought by Anima? But not for long did Animus allow himself to be reduced to this inferior position; very soon did he show his true nature – vain, pedantic and tyrannical.

Anima is an ignoramus and a fool, she has never been to school; whereas Animus knows a heap of things, he has read a heap of things in books . . . all his friends say that it is impossible to be a better talker . . . Anima has no longer the right to say a word . . . he knows better than she what she wants to say. Animus is not faithful, but that does not prevent him being jealous that all the fortune belongs to Anima, and that he is a beggar, and lives on what she gives him. So he is endlessly exploiting and tormenting her to get money out of her . . . She stays silently at home to do the cooking and clean the house as best she can . . . But something strange had happened . . . One day Animus came in unexpectedly . . . he heard Anima singing to herself behind closed doors a curious song, something he did not know; there was no way of discovering the notes, or the words, or the key – a strange and wonderful song. Since then he has slyly tried to make her repeat it, but Anima pretends not to understand. She is silent as soon as he looks at her. The soul is silent when the mind looks at it. Then Animus thinks he will play a trick on her; he takes steps to make her think he is not present . . . little by little Anima reassures herself, she looks here and there, she listens, she sighs, she thinks herself alone, and noiselessly she goes and opens the door to her divine lover.[1]

The idea that the heart 'opens the door to her divine lover' in prayer, agrees beautifully with 'softness, and peace, and joy, and love, and bliss'.

We use prayer as a means to an end – as an engine, a plummet, a spear, etc. We pray in order to shift things, to get things done. Prayer, we believe, energizes action and therefore we will go on praying. But we cannot in all honesty associate those practical, bread-and-butter applications of prayer with 'softness . . . and bliss'. What level of prayer is Herbert describing? There is such a thing as 'pure' prayer offered to the Father 'in spirit and truth' which 'the Father seeks' (John 4.23, 24). Pure in the sense that it has no strings attached, it isn't after anything in return, it is more interested in God than in his goods. It is a glorifying thanksgiving, a simplicity of prayer, which answers God for his love. Von Balthasar comments on such prayer that 'love desires no other reward than love in return; and so, in return for his love God wants nothing but our love'.[2]

A moment's reflection on the motivations of our prayer-life may reveal how self-interested much of it is, and in that sense how 'un-pure' prayer can be. What we are calling 'pure' prayer is at the service of the divine love. It is in harmony with it: a simple adoration in which we tell the Lord that we understand what he is saying, his gift to us in Christ, and the love with which he loves us. We tell him that by his love we have been awakened to love, and how we long to love him more. In 'pure' prayer we will attempt (however poorly) to make a sincere answer to his word in order to show that we have understood him. Of all things, a lover desires the beloved to understand what he is saying.

There will be, therefore, an element of 'pointlessness' about pure prayer because it is a giving thanks when there is nothing to be gained by doing so. Thus it was for the healed leper who returned to seek Jesus his healer, 'praising God in a loud voice. He threw himself at Jesus' feet and thanked him' (Luke 17.15–16); also the healed blind man on his knees before Jesus crying, 'Lord, I believe' (John 9.38). In both cases (and the New Testament is full of examples) their exuberant praise was, from a practical point of view, a waste of time and energy. They each already had their healing. Pure glorifying prayer is utterly uncalculating with no trace of capitalizing on the grace of God or channelling it even towards worthy ends. But how very modern is Judas' indignation at a woman's 'pointless' outpourings of love in her 'expensive perfume' lavished on Jesus' feet. There is such a contemporary ring to Judas' pseudo-compassionate, efficient, business-like and 'reasonable' protest, 'Why wasn't this perfume sold and the money given to the poor? It was worth a year's wages' (John 12.1–5).

Quite unknowingly Judas defines a quality of pure glorifying prayer, which arouses 'softness, and peace, and joy, and love, and bliss' in the heart: a year's wages 'wasted' in two minutes of adoration. Judas was not to know of the immense movements of love and social action, which were to flow from people energized, like Mary on that occasion, by passionate love for Christ. Pure prayer, of

Mary's sort, may well appear senseless, wasteful, irrelevant, and ineffectual to a world engaged in its big, urgent projects: why spend valuable time on your knees when you could be out on the street collecting for famine relief in the Sudan? Why 'waste' thousands on the church spire, money that could better be used helping the poor and needy?

Our answer to both questions is 'yes' to love-in-action, but our life depends upon the priority of prayer that frankly has no point to it other than to adore the divine lover. Such prayer, therefore, comes *before* work, mission, service and social programmes. You will have noticed what is missing in that love poem between the Lord and his people, the Song of Songs. The two lovers – bride and bridegroom – are childless; together in the enclosed garden of their love, and there are no children. It is a picture of the worshipper whom 'the Father seeks'. The fact is he wants us for ourselves and not simply for what we can do for him. He does not call us to himself to be fertilizer for the great mission of the Kingdom. No doubt the 'children' of fruitful service will follow as a consequence of our union with him, but first he wants our love in response to his love. At this level of communion with him in prayer, this utterly simple, 'pure' level, expect awareness of 'softness . . . and bliss'.

It is the form of prayer that Jesus praised above all others: contemplative-meditative prayer as exemplified by Mary, Martha's sister. However irksome to our natural activism, we must side with Mary who 'sat at the Lord's feet listening to what he said', while Martha was 'distracted by all the preparations' (Luke 10.38–42). Listening-contemplative-meditative prayer must be given first place in the spiritual discipline of our personal lives, because listening (not doing) is the first worship God requires of us: 'Hear now (*Shema!*) O Israel'. Action – fruitful within the purposes of God – will follow on from listening-prayer, but without it we will take ourselves far too seriously, and shoulder too many burdens in our own strength.

Far from becoming passive and detached from the action, contemplative-prayer people are wise and effective because first they listened to the Lord. Lady Julian described the illuminating and revelatory influence of the Spirit: 'For it is God's good pleasure to reign in our understanding blissfully, and sit in our soul restfully, and to dwell in our soul endlessly, us all working into him.' Only in this way will we learn to recognize the presence of the Lord, in meditative-prayer, pure and glorifying. Without it we haven't a hope of recognizing him in the midst of a hectic world.

Also it is by the cultivation of contemplative-prayer that we are able to fulfil the puzzling command to 'pray continually' (1 Thessalonians 5.17) with what is literally 'unceasing prayer'. Puzzling, because very difficult to do (as well as being dangerous and probably illegal) in a hectic life of handling machines, and babies, driving a car, and crossing busy roads. Some recommend that we can obey the injunction by practising the discipline of the Eastern 'Jesus Prayer', in ceaseless repetition ('Lord Jesus Christ, Son of God, have mercy on me a sinner'). Others warn that they find the process disturbing and slightly schizophrenic. But Mary's meditative prayer, pondering the Lord's words and love, brings with it a picture of the presence of the Lord forming in the memory for the imagination to work on. In that sense we 'pray continually' in that the Lord is everywhere present to our inner world.

The result, says Urs von Balthasar, is 'rather in the way a man is always and everywhere influenced by the image of the woman he loves',[3] which brings us back to 'softness, and peace, and joy, and love, and bliss'.

CHAPTER 11

Exalted Manna,
gladness of the best

When next you dine at your favourite Israeli restaurant, try the manna. You might reflect on its significance to the prophetic mind, and how George Herbert could ever utter 'manna' in the same breath as 'gladness of the best'. 'A sweet, sticky substance produced by a number of insects that suck the tender twigs of tamarisk bushes in the desert region of Sinai. This "honeydew excretion" falls to the ground where in the hot desert air, the drops quickly evaporate, leaving a solid residue . . . early risers can gather the substance for food.' Herbert is suggesting that this unlikely wilderness survival snack holds the key to prayer.

The surprise of linking manna to prayer is cushioned if instead of original, 'neat', manna, the chef has served up a confection known as 'manna from heaven'. It is made by dissolving the 'honeydew excretion' in hot water, straining out the bits of twigs and insects, then cooking it to a thick porridge and adding chopped almonds. One Jewish cookbook comments that 'a pudding made with the manna cooked to a soft cream is eaten with thick buffalo cream'.[1] Almonds and cream indeed! Not according to the Exodus account of Israel's trek through the desert (Exodus 16.11–16). Yet the psalmist called manna 'the grain of heaven . . . bread of angels' (Psalm 78.24, 25).

Far from being simply a wayside snack to keep Israel fuelled on her journey to Canaan, the whole purpose of the journey was to bring the people to the manna!

Remember how the LORD your God led you all the way in the desert these forty years, to humble you and to test you in order to know what was in your heart, whether or not you would keep his commands. He humbled you, *causing you to hunger and then feeding you with manna,* which neither you nor your fathers had known, to teach you that man does not live on bread alone but on every word that comes from the mouth of the LORD (Deuteronomy 8.2–3).

So the great forty-year wilderness trek was one long lesson in practical trust.

What an incredibly dangerous teaching method that was to risk bringing the people (including children and the elderly, the pregnant and the sick) to the edge of starvation 'and then feeding them with manna'. What could be so important to merit such a drastic lesson? They were discovering the answer to another question: *by what does man live?* At stake is our integrity as people created to be satisfied by joyful communion with the living Lord (we are to see ourselves included in Israel's drama). Atoms buzz and bleep, birds fly, moles dig – each acts true to its nature. We, made in the image of God, have a nature designed to know and enjoy God for ever. Failure to do so would be a personal catastrophe for any individual. We are gifted for delight in God's company, able to converse with him in the Spirit, to grow into fulness of life through obedience to his mind expressed in his word.

If we are by nature hungering, greedy and acquisitive people, then so be it. Only let us be wise enough to turn to the one source able to satisfy our deepest longings, which is the life of God:

> They feast in the abundance of your house;
> you give them drink from your river of delights.
> For with you is the fountain of life . . .
>
> (Psalm 36.8–9)

Charles Williams writes that 'this should be our covetousness and our desire; for this only no greed is too great, as this only can satisfy the greatest greed'.[2]

But that glorious invitation is distorted by the fantasy of sin. 'Sin', said George Herbert, 'is flat opposite to th' Almighty.' In a bizarre contradiction (the devil is clever with smoke and mirrors) we misread our own restlessness and allow ourselves to be fobbed off with mere things. We hide within God's gifts in order to protect ourselves from him. Thus we choose not only to be grateful for 'bread', but to live 'by bread *alone*', which is demonic for it shatters a human being's dependence upon the true source of life in God.

No sooner are we flourishing within life's good plenty than our innate atheism kicks in: we can live by bread *alone*, money *alone*, power *alone*, sex *alone* and so on. Practical atheism of that common sort is not the invention of modern materialism; it was alive and well in the Sinai desert around 1200 BC.

Apparently God reckoned it was worth every minute of those forty years to wean Israel (she was the representative human family) off the deadly fantasy of life 'by bread alone'. He initiates a crisis. With the goodies of Egypt far behind them, and the relative security and prosperity of Canaan a long way ahead of them, he takes Israel into the laboratory of the wilderness. There, away from the shops, the stock market, and the cinemas; away from theoretical classroom religion, life focuses down to a terrible simplicity: can God be trusted with our lives? Is he as good as his word? Is the Lord among us or not? (Exodus 17.7).

The crisis strips away the customary scaffolding, those things on which we depend and by which we live; the stuff to which we cling in place of God. At this moment either we leap on to God's promises like drowning people clinging to a life raft, or we are lost. The Japanese character for 'crisis' is a combination of the characters for 'danger' and 'opportunity' (or 'promise'). Crisis is therefore not the end of opportunity but in reality only its beginning. For Israel (and ourselves in Israel's experience) the food crisis was the beginning of the opportunity to swap her double-mindedness, her compromise, her lukewarm half-heartedness, and to come clean with God. Suddenly the mirage of life 'by bread alone' can be seen for what it is over against life by obedience 'to every word that comes from the mouth of the Lord'. At that moment God leads his hungry people to the manna.

Manna is, therefore, the food of believers who risk everything on God. He will preserve and nourish them with his own food, 'the grain of heaven . . . bread of angels'. That is the promise and only by living experimentally can we prove it. Because this decisiveness is so enriching, God is forever moving us into situations of crisis that confront us with danger and opportunity. Testing, searching, challenging, clarifying, crisis is the point of growth. There God feeds his people with his manna. Urs von Balthasar writes on this process:

> Nothing plays a greater role in God's pedagogical art than the shift from one to the other extreme. No sooner have we learned something halfway and begun to grasp it than (Oh, shock!) out of the warm bath and into the cold! This is meant to ensure that we do not settle into any situation but remain pliable, and to make us recognize that true insight does not come from what we have grasped but from ever greater readiness and deeper obedience.[3]

Manna is the strange food of God encountered by people on the move in response to his word. It is, says George Herbert, not manna-on-the-ground, under those tamarisk bushes at Sinai, but '*Exalted* Manna', for it is the life, grace and power of our risen and ascended Lord Jesus Christ.

Prayer is a Bedouin who traverses the wilderness in obedience to God's word, looking to Christ, our exalted manna, for sustenance. Prayer is our response to those moments of crisis, the danger that we might live by bread alone and the opportunity to choose to live instead by God's word. By prayer we open up the crisis to Christ's power and love, in total honesty about our fears and confusions and all the 'what ifs?' raised by crisis. By prayer the exalted manna passes into our bodies, hearts and minds and amazingly we find ourselves going joyfully on our way with our Lord.

Manna was a *providential* blessing in itself. It was a natural occurrence, the product of insects, tamarisk bush, and desert climate. It was *providential* in that God saw to it that his travelling people encountered the natural phenomenon of manna when they needed it most. Therefore, our prayers will be alert to the providential dimension of Christ's provision. Time after time we have apparently chance meetings with other people by whom we are helped: 'I missed my usual bus and on the next one I sat down next to someone who just happened to be reading . . .' How many times do we hear, or overhear, a few words that seize our attention, for they speak to our situation? A young man told me about a time of real personal crisis in his life when he was working in Egypt. A lapsed Christian, he was desperately, if hopelessly, praying that God would give him some sort of guidance about his future. At his wits' end, he wandered into the only Christian church in that town, even though it was Egyptian speaking, which he did not understand. He described to me his misery sitting there with a torrent of unintelligible Egyptian pouring out all around him, shut into his worries about his future, when it happened. Half way through his sermon, the preacher paused and said in perfect English, 'I know not what the future holds, but I know who holds the future' – a line from a well-known old hymn. Manna from heaven. God's providence at work. He takes an Egyptian preacher's sermon preparation and causes it to intersect with a young Englishman desperately seeking guidance: a rather spectacular instance of a process that is happening all the time around us.

By prayer we hold our lives and circumstances open to God's providential manna. We will be sensitive to the mysterious confluence of people, circumstances and provision, which open up the future for us. The Lord appears in the midst of our thoughts and we discover, to our astonishment, that we are strangely joyful. I love especially the references to providential 'exalted manna' in Gregory Petrov's hymn, the Akathist of Thanksgiving. In his crisis he had chosen obedience to Christ over Marxist atheism and spent years in Stalin's terrible Siberian camps because of it. His hymn is a torrent of ecstatic praise and prayer, including these lines:

Glory to you for your unceasing care for me,
Glory to you for providential meetings with people,
Glory to you for the providential coincidence of circumstances,
Glory to you for beneficial premonitions,
Glory to you for warnings of a secret voice,
Glory to you for revelations asleep and awake.

And, most startling:

Glory to you, ruining our unprofitable plans.[4]

To our sceptical friends our decision to pin our hopes on the exalted manna of God's providential care is bewildering. Just look at what it did for Gregory Petrov! He had to endure life in the appalling frozen Siberian wasteland. We answer, yes, look what it did for him. Look at his sense of mastery, and mysterious serenity, over his circumstances. His food, George Herbert is saying, has all the nourishment and 'gladness of the best'. We are familiar with the disappointment of the second rate and the disillusionment of the mediocre, they are our familiar diet. But exalted manna is gladness of the best. This, too, is entirely an experimental discovery. The Lord may yet have to lead us into a wilderness, or 'Siberian', crisis before we prove its qualities for ourselves, and then we will have a story to tell.

CHAPTER 12

Heaven in ordinary,
man well dressed

No one gets out of bed well dressed. As my wife explains to me frequently, a smart appearance doesn't simply arrive with the morning
post. It requires careful preparation, time spent in front of the
mirror, and I can only believe her. So when George Herbert says
that prayer is 'man well dressed' I am inclined to think he means the
necessary prayer before prayer, preparation for prayer; the act of
praying oneself into prayer.

Who of us would question the need for it? Left to ourselves, isn't
it true that most of us are spiritually mostly asleep most of the time?
Our inner life settles easily into a no-man's-land mood, about as
vibrant as yesterday's leftover porridge – a dull cold stodge. All we
can do at that point is to be frank and un-clever with God about
our jadedness and boredom, and ask him to do for us what we
cannot do for ourselves – give the desire and energy to pray, shift us
out of our death.

Experience and experiment over the years evolves strategies for
entering into prayer. Some folk reclaim their inner world first thing
in the day by reading a psalm or meditating on a set daily passage
of scripture. Others, I am assured, sing or listen to spirit-warming
music, they may contemplate a picture or an icon or a candle flame.
We each must find our own way and having done so share our
findings with one another. So here goes: my own strategy for
moving from stodge to 'well dressed' for prayer involves reaching for
a battered ring-folder. It contains pages of dog-eared, tea-stained,
and much scribbled upon 'prayers before prayer' meditations and
poems. With these I make some progress towards getting my soul
together and 'well dressed' for worship.

The pages speak with the familiar voices of old friends (we have been through a lot together). They contain little that is new, for I'm not looking for novel thoughts at that moment; rather they work like a wise old border collie rounding up my flock of unruly thoughts, enough to allow prayer to happen.

Thus I may (and this really comes down to a matter of managing moods) turn first thing to a lovely reminder of the nature and value of this self-soul, which God has conferred upon me ('Lord, how could you give yourself to me if you had not first given me to myself?'), in the Hebrew hymn 'Song at Daybreak':

> I shall give thanks to the Lord, who tests the heart, when the morning stars sing together.
>
> Take care of the soul: she is turquoise, agate and jasper. Her light is like the light of the sun, like the light of seven mornings as she was hewn from the throne of glory...
>
> May God find her wrapped in Prayer shawl and frontlets, always dressed like a bride, morning after morning.
>
> ... If a man does not keep his soul alive, how will he be worthy of the light of the morning?[1]

Those words illuminate the moment; they are a call that I snap out of my lazy self-absorption and get 'well dressed' to go to God in prayer. They say 'pastor yourself' in the sense of taking responsibility for one's own interior life.

Those thoughts lead on to the next page in the folder and perhaps settle on a prayer from the Gaelic inviting the Lord to pour his life under the deepest roots of the believer's life, the place where the desires, thoughts and motivations come to birth and where the outcomes are decided:

> Holy God, loving Father of the Word everlasting,
> Grant me to have of thee this living prayer –
>
> Lighten my understanding,
> Kindle my will,

Begin my doing,
Incite my love,
Strengthen my weakness,
Enfold my desire

– Amen.

I keep a sequence of prayers and meditations (the Gaelic prayer is both) for as long as they 'work', changing them – removing some, adding others – when they no longer seem to turn over and ignite the engine. My interest is not aesthetic but entirely practical and pastoral. Certain of them leap off the page however many times I read them, such as Urs von Balthasar's outburst, which reaches me like a slap in the face every time: 'What manners! To receive God's daily visit not in the living room of one's soul but in the kitchen or hallway!'[2]

More formal prayers-before-praying, prayers for entering prayer, are also helpful in dressing the spirit for communion with the Father, such as this one from E. Milner-White's book *My God – My Glory*:

MY GOD and Father,
> help me to pray
>> as my first work,
>> my unremitting work,
>> my highest, finest, and dearest work;
> as the work I do for you, and by you,
>> and with you,
>> for other of your children and for the whole world.

LORD, help me to pray;
>> to desire to pray,
>> to delight to pray.
Make all my supplication joyful with faith,
>> joyful with hope,
>> joyful with love:
joyful with your own Spirit interceding with me,
>> urgent with his yearning behind my inattention,
>> wide with his wisdom behind my dim-sightedness,
>> burning with his fire behind my lukewarmth:

joyful in the fellowship of the prayers of your saints,
   and of your whole Church, above, below;
through him who in heaven makes intercession continually,
   your Son Jesus Christ our Lord.

LORD, you who give the will to pray,
  make my prayer good,
 humble, ardent and effectual,
   by the kindling of your Spirit;
   by the sincerity of my soul,
    its conformity to your will,
    its order to your glory;
   by the devotion of my heart,
   the strong tranquillity of its faith,
   the wide charity of its desires,
   the fervour of its love,
    and the importunity of its pleading;
   through Jesus Christ our Lord.[3]

Although we may come to God 'well dressed' in prayer that of itself can never be the grounds of our confidence. Herbert's apparently quaint and homely metaphor is a ticking bomb and when it sinks into our understanding and explodes its meaning, the gospel is revealed! We dress up, and are met by the God who dresses down: prayer is 'heaven in ordinary, man well dressed'. A couple of weeks ago, I witnessed a nice illustration of what Herbert is saying.

The Queen visited our small town. I have here several photos of the occasion to send to an old lady in Mexico who is a great fan of the Queen. In them people are smiling, the policewoman is smart and watchful; the mayor looks satisfied if slightly burdened, a group of Morris dancers are clearly in top form. But it's the children I am most intrigued by. I wonder what they made of the occasion? Were they a shade disappointed? I ask this because although the market place was thoroughly 'well dressed' for the visit, the Queen arrived 'in ordinary'. She looked like anyone's grandmother, dressed in neat 'sensible' clothes for enjoying a day out among friends with a decent lunch not far off. Not a tiara to be seen, no glitter, no great coach or Household Cavalry ready to haul local rowdies off to the Tower. You could almost hear the four-year-olds muttering to each other 'Is that it?'

When town 'well dressed' encountered Queen 'in ordinary' it made for a relaxed, happy, informal day. The dazzle of majesty didn't get in the way of real meeting. 'Man well dressed' is nothing more than our duty, the respect we owe our creator; 'heaven in ordinary' is all grace and love and divine self-emptying. Our confidence, joy and peace in meeting with God is held in the phrase 'heaven in ordinary' and in the answer to our question, 'How ordinary is God's ordinary?'

As ordinary as the incarnation of our Lord Jesus, who 'made himself nothing, taking the very nature of a servant' (Philippians 2.7). The splendour of his majestic glory was not allowed to distance him from us; he came as close to us as one of us. The God, who in his blazing holiness is a terrifying prospect for sinful people, has done the unthinkable. He has crossed over to our side in Christ. Not merely in a symbolical gesture but in utterly real identification and solidarity with us. Now he stands among his people, 'in ordinary', extending all the achievement of his life, death and resurrection to cover and to include us. He is our saving brother 'Jesus' (Hebrews 2.10–18). How 'ordinary'? He clothed himself with the reality of our flesh and all its weakness, then redeemed it, us and all mankind from within our flesh. As the Church Fathers delighted to proclaim, 'what Christ did not assume he could not heal'. He assumed, took on to himself, all of our nature and flesh ('in ordinary') in order to heal it, us, completely from within.

Just ponder what Christ's 'in ordinary' means as we approach him 'well dressed' in prayer. He, God, is as near to us as our own nature, as the breath in our bodies. There is no gap between God and us. To close the gap for ever, God in Christ clothed himself with our nature; we clothe ourselves with his nature as children of God. We are 'in Christ' and Christ is 'in me'. We could explore this astonishing truth for the remainder of the book; instead we will allow George Herbert to summarize it in what I find to be his most profound poem, 'Aaron'.

Turning the Diamond

A Christian priest is about to lead the congregation in worship. He comes prepared by prayer to pray. He is at his best, 'well dressed':

1.   Holiness on the head,
          Light and perfections on the breast,
  Harmonious bells below, raising the dead
        To lead them unto life and rest:
            Thus are true Aarons dressed.

Then the truth about himself as a sinner breaks in upon him with a devastating sense of his utter weakness and inability to lead anyone to God in worship:

2.   Profaneness in my head,
        Defects and darkness in my breast,
  A noise of passions ringing me for dead
        Unto a place where is no rest:
           Poor priest thus am I dressed.

He is saved, as we all are saved, by the fact that Christ came 'in ordinary' to take our nature to himself and to bestow his nature on us. 'In Christ' means Christ adding himself to us totally, in every respect; 'head, heart, breast, music':

3.   Only another head
        I have, another heart and breast,
  Another music, making live not dead,
        Without whom I could have no rest:
           In him I am well dressed.

Life, communion and ministry are now ours because they are Christ's, we are in union with him, one with him:

4.   Christ is my only head,
        My alone only heart and breast,
  My only music, striking me ev'n dead;
        That to the old man I may rest,
          And be in him new dressed.

Heaven in ordinary, man well dressed
> So holy in my head,
> Perfect and light in my dear breast,
> My doctrine tuned by Christ (who is not dead,
> But lives in me while I do rest),
> Come people; Aaron's dressed.

Prayer is 'heaven in ordinary, man well dressed'.

CHAPTER 13

The Milky Way,
the bird of Paradise

Approaching the full circle of Herbert's diamond as we turn it in the light, his 'inspired litany . . . This zodiac of marvels' (page 2), we meet images of 'near-hallucinogenic intensity'. But the author isn't simply handing around mystical cannabis when he describes prayer under the ravishing metaphors of 'the Milky Way, the bird of Paradise'. Those are ecstatic images – in the sense that we are taken out of our usual thought by them – but Christian ecstasy is never a flight from reality, rather the opposite. Like the shimmering and radiant effect of bright sunlight on water, Christian ecstasy arises out of our being 'in Christ' who is the Lord of all reality. Movement into Christ is movement into reality.

Christ indwells his people, who indwell him by the Holy Spirit. It is a relationship which places us in vital connection with the One who even at this moment is speaking all creation into being, and holding it in life (Hebrews 1.1–4; Colossians 1.15–20). We are thereby mysteriously but truly related to 'All things', they are our rightful sphere by virtue of our union with Christ their Lord. An incredible statement of our status in Christ runs:

All things are yours, whether Paul or Apollos or Cephas or the world or life or death or the present or the future – all are yours, and you are of Christ, and Christ is of God. (1 Corinthians 3.21–3)

One thing is made crystal clear by those words: no longer can we conceive of 'in Christ and Christ in me' as a purely internalized, privatized affair concerned mainly, if not exclusively, with our own inner world. If Christ the Lord of 'All things' dwells in you and you in him, then you have dealings and connections with everything else. Therefore no sooner has George Herbert satisfied us concerning the nearness of Christ, and prayer as the language of our personal intimacy with him ('Heaven in ordinary...') than he sends us rocketing out to the boundaries of our estate, 'All things ... the world ...' Except he suggests those farthest limits not by equations or formulae, but in two utterly beautiful things located way out there in the distance.

Prayer as reaching up into the immensities of space is symbolized by the lovely, hazy, stream of rich star-fields flowing through Cassiopeia and across Orion, which we call the Milky Way. And to indicate the boundaries where knowledge emerges from mystery and discovery takes over from hiddenness, Herbert invokes a creature of mythic elusiveness and beauty – for a seventeenth-century Englishman located on Salisbury Plain – from the jungles of the strange and fascinating East: the bird of Paradise. An old authority describes it in the following way:

Of the Paradise-birds we know but little, for they are almost entirely confined to New Guinea, and a few neighbouring islands in the Indian seas, inhabited by wild tribes, with whom travellers have but little communication. These people catch the Paradise-birds and dry their skins, which they barter with ships passing along the coast. It was for a long time believed, by ignorant persons, that they had no legs, for they were never seen alive, excepting when flying across from one island to another, the natives always bringing dead specimens for sale, without the legs, possibly because they thought they looked better without them, in many species the leg being coarse, and unbecoming a bird in every other respect so exquisitely beautiful. It is quite impossible to describe their beauty, or give even a faint idea of it without coloured representations; and few of the most favoured of the feathered race can rival them in the gorgeous variety and singularity of their splendid dress. Some are ornamented with light projecting tufts, of a fine downy substance, while others have plumes and tendrils flying out in every direction, like pennants and streamers, while their bodies glisten with the most dazzling and resplendent hues, changing from crimson and gold to the most delicate green or purple, according as the sun's rays fall upon the feathers. It is said that they frequent the most retired spots of the thick woods of their native country.[1]

It seems therefore that prayer as a star galaxy and as an exotic bird is a beguiling way of claiming 'All things . . . the world . . .' as the domain of prayer and worship. It is saying that everything that exists should be raised up to God in thanksgiving for his glory. Eric Mascall describes our work of prayer like this:

There are things – the most vital things of all – which the Church does for the world, which the world cannot do for itself. And this is all the more important at a time when so many of the tasks which the Church did for the world when the world had not learnt to do them for itself are now being done by the world very successfully – education, medical care and the rest of the social services. The one thing that the Church can do for the world which the world will never be able to do for itself, at least until the kingdoms of this world have themselves become the kingdom of God and of his Christ, is to offer the world to God to be transfigured by his grace and to be taken into his life.[2]

I find that a wonderfully liberating vision of how a Christian prays in and for the world. What is the purpose of your church within its parish or district? Many things: loving service, worship, evangelism, teaching, youth ministry and so on. But supremely, as an overarching definition, God has called the congregation into being in that place for the priestly work of offering it to God by prayer and worship: to do for it what it doesn't think of doing for itself, which is to seek its renewal and transfiguration in God. Such prayer reaches far beyond the limits of the church.

A friend once told me that when he gave thanks for his food in a restaurant he extended his silent prayer to include everyone in the place: as their brother, and on their behalf, just in case God should go un-thanked for his gifts! He had hit upon a profound aspect, perhaps the central one, of a Christian's function within a largely unbelieving society.

Our relationship to the culture at the present time is best described by the Greek word 'diaspora' meaning 'dispersion' (1 Peter 1.1, 2). Christians are spread and scattered around society, a minority everywhere. Nowhere do we have numbers and authority enough to stamp the Christian ideal upon society and its culture. Some talk nostalgically of a return to the 'old times' when the Christian Church enjoyed power and status, but 'Christendom' shows no sign of making a come-back. Indeed, for whatever reasons, our influence in public life looks set to decline further in terms of numerical proportion. In other words we are approaching a state of affairs normative in the New Testament, a 'diaspora' Church, a Christian minority scattered (like salt, or seed) among a non-Christian or at best a nominally Christian society. Salt is also 'in the minority' within the food on your plate; yeast also is small to the point of invisibility within the dough; plant a seed in the ground and it is swallowed up out of sight. But look at their transforming effect.

As Christians called to live in this present time of 'dispersion' our chief ministry will be to lift up our local world in our prayers (our family, street, place of work, entertainment) for the glory of the Father who gives life. Look out of your window. Hopefully the folk in the houses you see also pray, but maybe they don't. In love and in solidarity, do for them what they may not think of doing for themselves, seeking God's transforming blessing by prayer. As 'priest' in your street (1 Peter 2.9, 10) offer it to God for his perfect will. Incidentally, you will notice how this attitude of representative, vicarious praise quite alters the way you view people.

We are suggesting that prayer as 'the Milky Way, the bird of Paradise' will open up our interests and prayers to take in all life. This is the wisdom and subversive power of 'diaspora' life. Christians are scattered all over society, yet placed there by God for his purposes: cells of prayer and worship, claiming the neighbourhood for God's transfiguring blessing.

You have long since discovered how compressed and concentrated Herbert's apparently simple images are. It is necessary to 'move in' with his metaphors before they yield their content. So I ask: why these two unusual things, the galaxy of stars and the exotic bird? Did Herbert smile to himself when he saw them side by side on the paper in front of him? I hope so, for they make me smile every time I read them. And I am sure they make children smile. 'The Milky Way' – what luck! To think that someone had the good sense to name the 100,000 million stars of our galaxy after a chocolate bar! And who thought to call that magical bird after 'Paradise' (meanings within meanings, within meanings)?

What has Herbert hidden for us within the two images? Both are stunning in their exotic and elusive beauty. They suggest prayer as a looking at the God of indescribable and holy loveliness, the fount of all joy and love and delight. A suggestion also of what has been called Christian hedonism. David Ford writes:

> Praise is about pleasure. Christianity has been understandably reticent about the joy, bliss, delight and sheer pleasure at its heart. But it is so, simply because its God is the God of joy. Christian hedonism is the holy intoxication of pleasing and being pleased by God, and that sums up the experience of praise.[3]

Prayer as the Milky Way, the bird of Paradise is a break-through to contemplative prayer, and to fresh realizations. Take Job, for example:

> And these are but the outer fringe of his works;
> How faint the whisper we hear of him!
> Who then can understand the thunder of his power?
>
> (26.14)

> My ears had heard of you
> but now my eyes have seen you.
> Therefore I despise myself
> and repent in dust and ashes.
>
> (42.5–6)

For those who prefer their prayer plain, simple, and direct these references to contemplative prayer may seem too mysterious. Fair enough, but God is mystery and, as someone has well said, 'The true alternative is not mystery or clarity, but mystery or absurdity.' With his 'the Milky way, the bird of paradise' George Herbert is laying a trail for our prayer into the mystery of God.

CHAPTER 14

Church-bells beyond the stars heard, the soul's blood

Herbert's images are like one of those Russian dolls that contain dolls within dolls. His uncanny compression of ideas needs careful unpacking. So, prayer is said to be like 'church-bells beyond the stars heard' which at first glance suggests that when the bells of Herbert's church, St Andrew's Bemerton, rang their call to worship the inhabitants of heaven took notice. Well, it would be disappointing to come all that way to be told something so unremarkable. We can easily believe that bells tolling in the local church tower on a Sunday morning are 'beyond the stars heard'. There are grounds for suspicion here, for Herbert is never that obvious! Open the Russian doll and out comes another suggesting the metaphor could be read the other way around.

It is not *our* church-bells that are heard 'beyond the stars', but *heaven*'s bells that are heard among us here in our world. Humbling though the thought is for people like ourselves who assume that nothing of worth happens unless we initiate it, the first call to prayer emanates from heaven. Our prayer-bells answer theirs 'on earth as it is in heaven'. Our churches are like an echo chamber for heavenly praise. The inhabitants of the sphere 'beyond the stars' are way ahead of us but they invite us to join with them in worshipping the Holy Trinity.

Herbert loved this perspective on prayer as already moving in the universe as we awake each morning (see chapters 2 and 9). We are never alone when praying; solitary worship is not possible since 'you have come to thousands upon thousands of angels in joyful assembly' (Hebrews 12.22), and our every moment is passed in their company. Sing, intercede, give thanks and the great congregation 'beyond the stars' open up their adoration to make room for ours. Thus in some of our services the scene is set:

> *Let us give thanks to the Lord our God . . .*
> Therefore with angels and archangels,
> And with all the company of heaven,
> We proclaim your great and glorious name . . .[1]

I think this truth dawned upon me one Ascension Day in Switzerland. We were on holiday in the village of Armden, which possessed two churches: one, a futuristic-looking building of the Swiss Reformed Church and the other, an old Catholic church. We planned to attend the service in the Reformed church, but before we did so I took a few minutes to look inside the Catholic church. Its walls were alive with medieval cartoons of gnarled saints, missionary heroes, and angels of such crude, primitive power that I almost expected to find feathers on the floor shed by a squadron of angels hurtling across the church. Then we went to 'our' church up the hill, as immaculate and perfect as a Swiss watch, except the comparison that came to mind was of a spotless, sterile operating theatre. A man in a black robe droned through a service for an impassive congregation; the walls were tastefully bare, except for one small expensive-looking tapestry. The inescapable feeling was of being utterly alone in that place as we tried vainly to lift our spirits on Ascension Day. Not a glimmer of 'angels and archangels, and with all the company of heaven' to accompany our worship.

George Herbert delighted in his conviction that Christ, heaven and creation are up and about the business of praise while we are still in our beds:

> I cannot ope mine eyes,
> But thou art ready there to catch
> My morning-soul and sacrifice . . .
>
> Teach me thy love to know;
> That this new light, which now I see,

> May both the work and workman show:
> Then by a sunbeam I will climb to thee.
>
>   ('Matins')

Jesus' resurrection set the pattern:

> Rise heart; thy Lord is risen. Sing his praise
>   Without delays,
> Who takes thee by the hand, that thou likewise
>   With him mayst rise:
> That, as his death calcined thee to dust,
> His life may make thee gold, and much more, just.

He ponders the fact that the disciples couldn't make it to the tomb before Christ was up!

> I got me flowers to straw thy way;
> I got me boughs off many a tree:
> But thou wast up by break of day,
> And brought'st thy sweets along with thee.
>
>   ('Easter')

In this image the 'church-bells beyond the stars' are the Holy Spirit pervading the life of the heavenly company, moving and orchestrating their worship. In that sphere God bestows his presence in three ways, says Austin Farrer:

> By a more visible providence, making the whole order of things the evident expression of an infinite goodness; by a more abundant grace, making the minds of his people transparent to his thought and their hearts to his love; by an incarnate presence with them in the glorified man, Jesus Christ.[2]

Farrer's comment hints at the teeming creativity of life in heaven. There is a popular view, put about by a falsely over-spiritualized idea of eternal life, that heaven will be predictable, boring, repetitious and very religious, a sort of perpetual vicarage tea party with breaks for prayer meetings. Or that it will be the sensual paradise of Islamic mythology, or the Hindu Nirvana of negated desires. But what sort of life and activity is suggested if 'a more abundant grace' makes the minds of God's people 'transparent to his thought and their hearts to his love'? Farrer adds: '[T]here is no coming to the end of God; the more we know of him and his ways, the more avenues will open up for further exploration.'[3]

The Holy Spirit calls out all heaven for the 'further exploration' into God. But in what sense can it be said that the Spirit's 'church-bells' are heard among us in the world? We can believe it because the same one Holy Spirit 'beyond the stars' also indwells his temple that is our bodies (1 Corinthians 6.19). The one Spirit creates one congregation of all in the universe who worship the Trinity. Spurgeon caught the heaven-on-earth dimension of our present life in his aphorism, 'If you have the minimum in the Christian life it will be enough to get you to heaven; if you have the maximum it will bring heaven to you on earth.' The maximum means we yield to the Spirit who orchestrates cosmic praise, ours on earth with theirs in heaven, taking both as one into Christ's ceaseless prayer before the Father.

It is in this sense that Christian worship is prophetic for it anticipates the consummation of 'all things' when Christ will 'fill the whole universe' (Ephesians 1.10 and 4.10). Already Christian worship points towards that transfiguration of the world; already in this life we are beginning to feel its tremors, church-bells beyond the stars are heard among us.

Shall we leave it at that, or is there still another doll hidden within our Russian doll? I believe there is. Consider the puzzling juxtaposition of 'the Milky Way' in the previous image, with 'beyond the stars'. If the stars (the Milky Way) are an image of prayer, what is Herbert hinting at when in the next line he takes us 'beyond the stars'? The more I reflect upon this I can only think he is with deliberate design signalling a very different aspect of prayer. Not that our thought about 'beyond the stars' as the heavenly sphere is 'wrong' (unless you think it is!) but here we have Herbert's wonderful pastoral honesty and his realism in spiritual things. 'Beyond the stars' goes through the ceiling of the Milky Way into an empty, dark, cold region. Is this Herbert's one reference in the sonnet to the experience of spiritual desolation, which the saints called 'the dark night of the soul'? His vision of prayer would be defective without it.

Prayer 'beyond the stars' refers to the times of spiritual emptiness and desolation we each of us have known to some extent. Like Job on his ash-heap, the Prodigal Son in his pigsty, Christ on Holy Saturday. It is an experience not much referred to from the pulpit, perhaps because it runs dead counter to the desires and ideals of our culture. On every hand, in countless TV programmes and their related spin-off bestsellers and periodicals, we are deluged with veneration for what is imagined to be the rich, inexhaustible resources of teeming self-sufficient interior life. But, if we are correct in our interpretation of Herbert's words, 'beyond the stars' shrewdly strips away those flattering deceptions about the self to reveal our true poverty before God.

Not only do those times of spiritual emptiness occur to most of us, it seems they are crucial to growth and progress. God in his love for us deals only in truth and reality when confronting us with our emptiness, our limited powers of understanding, and our perverse ability to confine ourselves in falsehood. Yet even then, *especially* then, we can hear the Spirit's voice, his 'church-bells' in the darkness. Thus Job survived his ash-heap, Jonah escaped his whale, the wayward son returned to the joy of his father's home, and Christ rose from the dead.

Elijah's 'beyond the stars' experience came in the shape of failed, empty guidance. Desperate for renewal he sat in his cave expecting God to speak to him in classic prophetic signs of the divine presence – the powerful wind, the earthquake, the fire. To his astonishment these impressive displays bore no word from God. Then came 'a gentle whisper' (1 Kings 19.12), which is a feeble translation of an enigmatic term meaning something like 'a small voice of still silence'. Rabbi Lawrence Kushner renders it as 'the soft, barely audible sound of almost breathing'. Elijah's prophetic charisma of discernment fell silent as he was stripped of powers associated with his special relationship with God. A shocking 'beyond the stars' moment for him, in order that he might go on to know God in a wholly new manner.

Prayer is also *'the soul's blood'*.

What blood is to the body, prayer is to the soul (see chapter 3, 'God's breath in man'). It would be foolish to describe physical blood as an 'aspect' of bodily life for that life is inconceivable without it. Blood is the essence of life. Similarly, to call prayer the 'soul's blood' is to claim for it a pervasive power and authority in our personal life as a child of God. The converse is only too apparent, for where prayer is neglected the sense of God's presence fades, we become spiritually enfeebled, burdened with unconfessed sin and anxieties, joy drains away and the Christian life declines into unreality. Or if we do retain the shape and outline of Christian life it lacks all grip and conviction.

No subtle or prolonged exposition of this image is required (I can detect no further Russian dolls within Russian dolls here!) other than to urge each other to 'pray without ceasing'. Let prayer surge and flow through us as naturally as the blood in our veins.

CHAPTER 15

The land of spices;
something understood

A final turn in the light and we are done. But what a haunting image our diamond has left us: prayer is 'the land of spices'.

In fact that 'land' reached from India, east to Malaysia and the necklace of Indonesian islands from Sumatra to Sulawesi. Entrepreneurial sea-going nations in the fifteenth century generated immense wealth by the Indo-Asian spice trade, when the value of a commodity could climb sixty-fold by the time it reached Europe: pepper, ginger, cinnamon, cardamoms, myrobalans (for dying and tanning), tamarind, amber, aloe-wood, cloves, nutmeg, mace, sandalwood, cottons and coconuts. A report from the period comments: 'From this it is to be understood that very great quantities must grow in the East and it need not be wondered that they are worth with us as much as gold.'[1] The term 'land of spices' represented also a culture, a state of mind in a time of tremendous energy, widening horizons, international collaboration as well as competition, new routes and discoveries, extraordinary advances in navigational skills, courageous explorations and intellectual expansion.

What does prayer as 'the land of spices' suggest to the imagination? Immense and rare riches from the East. It is an image of trafficking in the inexhaustible resources of Christ; a drawing upon his person, life, death and resurrection, his gift to us of the outpoured Holy Spirit, his ministry as mediator of the eternal covenant. It is an image of scripture's great obsession:

Thanks be to God for his indescribable gift! . . . For you know the grace of our Lord Jesus Christ, that though he was rich, yet for your sakes he became poor, so that you through his poverty might become rich ... to grasp how wide and long and high and deep is the love of Christ, and to know this love that surpasses knowledge – that you may be filled to the measure of all the fulness of God ... his incomparably great power for us who believe. That power is like the working of his mighty strength, which he exerted in Christ when he raised him from the dead ... Christ, in whom are hidden all the treasures of wisdom and knowledge. (2 Corinthians 9.15 and 8.9; Ephesians 3.18 and 1.19–20; Colossians 2.2–3)

Those are a small sample of scripture's celebration of God's gift of his Son to the world. Prayer in the Holy Spirit opens up the believer to the immensities of Christ's presence.

Enormous courage and skill were required by the seamen who brought cargoes from the Spice Islands to Europe. Eyewitness accounts, rumours, charts and ships of themselves could never transfer those exotic commodities from Sulawesi to Southampton. Set sail and stick to the task. By prayer we go into Christ. We have his word that we will not return empty-handed. The danger lies not in any unwillingness on his part to give, but in the way we settle for spiritual pauperdom: half-starved, penniless and in rags – content (because in our hearts we believe it is where we belong) to stay on the street outside the Father's house looking in. Or, as our image suggests, content to scratch an existence in the chilly wastes of Siberia rather than rejoice in the lavish, lush hospitality of the Land of Spices. Yet, 'All things are yours'.

Several years ago a hugely popular TV show in the US worked by seeking out individuals who were unaware that they owned considerable wealth. In some cases a person was pretty near rock bottom in his circumstances. Imagine the emotions when the show's compère was able to prove to him that ten years earlier a distant wealthy relative had left him a fortune. There it was in such-and-such a bank awaiting collection. If prayer is 'the land of spices' why do we live on scraps from the local take-away?

Take the scriptures quoted earlier and go with them into Christ. Claim his promises. List them in a notebook; quote them to the

Lord in your prayers. 'My God will meet all your needs according to his glorious riches in Christ Jesus. To our God and Father be glory for ever and ever. Amen' (Philippians 4.19–20). But what about the time when you and others prayed so hard for that dear friend dying of cancer and nothing happened? Of course something 'happened' only you have no idea what it was 'happening' in your friend as you brought her to Christ for his healing. God alone knows what he did for her in response to your love and requests. He took hold of her in all the reality of her being, and the reality of her illness, and worked his will in her. We know this on the basis of Christ's own experience of the dilemma of undeserved suffering: 'Abba, Father, everything is possible for you. Take this cup from me. Yet not what I will, but what you will' (Mark 14.36).

Prayer as 'the land of spices' is not justification for a glib 'prosperity gospel' religion. It is an image of our unbreakable and irreversible union with Christ. 'For I am convinced that neither death nor life, neither angels nor demons, neither the present nor the future, nor any powers, neither height nor depth, nor anything else in all creation, will be able to separate us from the love of God that is in Christ Jesus our Lord' (Romans 8.38–9). Not least of the rich things that are ours from the 'land of spices' is a joyful freedom to take on whatever life or death can throw at us. That is the true healing, the true prosperity.

By prayer we travel to the 'land of spices' on behalf of others. Just as those Renaissance navigators and traders made their extraordinary trips with shopping lists matched against market demands back in Europe, so we go to our boundlessly generous Lord Jesus for the needs of the world. The Christian traffics between God and people. George MacDonald expressed this prayer ministry memorably:

> There is a chamber in God himself, into which none can enter but the one, the individual, the peculiar man – out of which chamber that man has to bring revelation and strength for his brethren. This is that for which he was made – to reveal the secret things of the Father.[2]

Prayer is '**something understood**'.

With a sigh and a click the diamond is returned to its box. It has shown many extraordinary aspects of prayer, dazzling and enigmatic, ecstatic and contemplative, delighting and puzzling. Each of them is an encouragement that we go on with prayer, do the experiment of faith, follow the promises into God, bring the world to him for his healing. None more so than in these final two words, George Herbert's sum total of the sonnet. Prayer is . . . 'something understood'.

It isn't prayer itself which is 'understood', rather in the act of praying to the Father, through Christ and in the power of the Holy Spirit an understanding dawns in our minds. It is the unity of all things in Christ. At last, the distressful fragmentation of the contemporary vision of life is healed, reconciled, unified in Christ. When we pray we have entrance into 'All things' because all life has its existence in Christ and we pray in him. Glance through the sonnet once more to remind yourself of the way prayer moves in all directions, explores into every secret sphere of the Spirit. As with each image in the sonnet, this final one also will prove itself to us as we do it. Pray, and receive the gift of 'something understood'.

References

CHAPTER 1 On finding a diamond

1, 2 Paterson, D. (ed.), *101 Sonnets*, Faber, London, 1999, p. 120.
3, 4 Heaney, S., *The Redress of Poetry*, Faber, London, 1995, p. 9.
5   Lewis, C. S., *An Experiment in Criticism*, Cambridge University Press, Cambridge, 2000, p. 93.

CHAPTER 2 Prayer the Church's banquet, Angels' age

1   von Balthasar, H. U., 'The Grain of Wheat', in *Aphorisms*, Ignatius Press, San Francisco, 1995, p. 126.
2   Boros, L., *Angels and Men*, Search Press, London, 1976, p. 35.
3   The Wisdom of Jesus the Son of Sirach (Ecclesiasticus).
4   von Balthasar, *Aphorisms*, p. 84.
5   MacDonald, G., *An Anthology*, ed. C. S. Lewis, Geoffrey Bles, London, 1946, p. 115.

CHAPTER 3 God's breath in man returning to his birth

1, 2 Kushner, L., *The Book of Words*, Jewish Lights Publishing, Vermont, 1993, pp. 27–9.
3   No.155 in *The Poems of Gerard Manley Hopkins*, Oxford University Press, Oxford, 1967.
4   von Balthasar, H. U., *Man in History*, Sheed and Ward, London, 1982, p. 264.

CHAPTER 4 The soul in paraphrase, heart in pilgrimage

1   Milosz, C. (ed.), *A Book of Luminous Things*, Harcourt Brace & Co., San Diego, 1996, p. 271.
2   von Balthasar, H. U., *Credo: Meditations on the Apostles' Creed*, T&T Clark, Edinburgh, 1990, p. 76.

3   Duffy, E., *The Stripping of the Altars*, Yale University Press, New Haven, 1992. Section on Pilgrimage from p. 190.

CHAPTER 6 Engine against the Almighty, sinner's tower

1   Farrer, A., *Said or Sung*, The Faith Press, 1960, p. 19.
2   John Donne. Quoted in J. Tobin (ed.), *The Complete English Poems of George Herbert*, p. 347.
3   Ellul, J., 'The Meaning of the City', Eerdmans, 1973, p. 16.

CHAPTER 7 Reversed thunder, Christ-side-piercing spear

1   Quoted in E. Duffy, *The Stripping of the Altars*, p. 237.

CHAPTER 8 The six-days world transposing in an hour

1   Hengel, M., *Crucifixion*, Fortress Press, Philadelphia, 1978, p. 19.
2   Attributed to St Patrick (386–460)
3   Williams, C., *Descent into Hell*, Eerdmans, Grand Rapids, 1999, p. 171.

CHAPTER 9 A kind of tune, which all things hear and fear

1   From the Vatican Decree on the Liturgy.
2, 3   Hay, D., *Religious Experience Today*, Mowbray, London, 1990, pp. 76, 77.
4   Kavanagh, P., 'Canal Bank Walk', in *The Complete Poems*, The Peter Kavanagh Hand Press, New York, 2001.
5   Richard Cook in *The Times*, 14 June 2001.
6   Hopkins, G. M., quoted in *Poems*, Oxford University Press, 1967, p. 263.

CHAPTER 10 Softness, and peace, and joy, and love, and bliss

1   Quoted in D'Arcy, M. C., *The Heart and Mind of Love*, Faber, London, 1954, p. 182.
2   von Balthasar, H. U., *Love Alone*, Sheed and Ward, London, 1982, p. 87.
3   von Balthasar, *Love Alone*, p. 89.

CHAPTER 11 Exalted Manna, gladness of the best

1   Roden, C., *The Book of Jewish Food*, Penguin, Harmondsworth, 1996, p. 22.
2   Williams, C., *War in Heaven*, Eerdmans, Grand Rapids, 1994, p. 104.
3   von Balthasar, *Aphorisms*, p. 109.
4   Archpriest Gregory Petrov, 'Akathist of Thanksgiving', translated by Mother Thekla, 1940.

CHAPTER 12 Heaven in ordinary, man well dressed

1   'Song at Daybreak', from *The Penguin Book of Hebrew Verse*, Penguin, Harmondsworth, 1981, p. 370.
2   von Balthasar, *Aphorisms*, p. 113.
3   Milner-White, E., *My God – My Glory*, SPCK, London, 1961, pp. 2, 6, 8.

CHAPTER 13 The Milky Way, the bird of Paradise

1   Stanley, E., *A Familiar History of Birds*, J. W. Parker, London, 1851, p. 193.
2   Mascall, E. L., *The Christian Universe*, DLT, London, 1967, p. 40.
3   Ford, D. F. and Hardy, D. W., *Jubilate: Theology in Praise*, DLT, London, 1984, p. 11.

CHAPTER 14 Church-bells beyond the stars heard, the soul's blood

1   From the Holy Communion Service (Rite A).
2   Farrer, A., *Saving Belief*, Hodder & Stoughton, London, 1964, p. 145.
3   Farrer, A., *A Celebration of Faith*, Hodder & Stoughton, 1970, p. 165.

CHAPTER 15 The land of spices; something understood

1   Quoted in Jardine, L., *Worldly Goods*, Macmillan, London, 1996, pp. 289, 298.
2   MacDonald, *An Anthology*.

Acknowledgements

The version of Herbert's poems used in this book is *The Complete English Poems of George Herbert*, Penguin Classics, Harmondsworth, 1991. This edition includes Isaac Walton's 'Life of George Herbert' and brief notes on the poems by the editor John Tobin.

Unless otherwise stated, Scripture quotations are taken from the HOLY BIBLE, NEW INTERNATIONAL VERSION. Copyright © 1973, 1978, 1984 by International Bible Society. Used by permission of Hodder & Stoughton Ltd, a member of the Hodder Headline Plc Group.

Extract (on page 78) from *The Notebooks and Papers of Gerard Manley Hopkins*, edited with notes and preface by Humphry House, Oxford University Press, 1937. Reprinted by permission of Oxford University Press.

Patrick Kavanagh, 'Canal Bank Walk', from *The Complete Poems of Patrick Kavanagh*, 2001, The Peter Kavanagh Hand Press, 35 Park Avenue, New York. Copyright 1972, 1996, 2001, Peter Kavanagh. With permission.

Extracts from Eric Milner-White's *My God – My Glory* are reproduced by permission of the Friends of York Minster.

Excerpt from *The Book of Words: Talking Spiritual Life, Living Spiritual Talk* © 1993 Lawrence Kushner (Woodstock, VT, USA: Jewish Lights Publishing). Order on-line at www.jewishlights.com. Permission granted by Jewish Lights Publishing, PO Box 237, Woodstock, VT 05091, USA.